"...Great read and I truly enjoyed it. Allowed me to see my mistakes and how to correct them. It's a hard truth that we must nurture our kids to what their potential and desires are not what we want them to be. The genius in Tri-C Parenting is in its simplicity. As parents we struggle to develop confident and productive young adults who are ready to go out into the world and find their passion. Dr. Rees gives us the tool to do just that. Tri-C Parenting should be the go to manual every parent should possess. Simply enlightening! "

- Ingrid Kohlmorgen, MD OB-GYN

"Parenting is hard.....Dr. Rees' highly informed approach to this crowded space is very welcome. Rather than providing lists of strategies and techniques, Dr. Rees helps the reader to understand fundamental and foundational concepts that will inform thoughtful parenting... (he) uses humor, gentle confrontation, and frank logic to help parents recognize past errors and future directions for improvement. I will enthusiastically recommend Tri-C Parenting to my patients!"

-Beth Lusby, PhD Child, Adolescent, & Adult Neuropsychologist and Clinical Psychologist.

Principal, Cornerstone Assessment and Guidance Center, LLC

"I loved the book. There were times that I actually laughed out loud....It was an easy read, and the application of the Tri-C strategies seem achievable. I appreciated the straight forward calling out of bad parenting choices, but then giving parents a framework for changing first their behavior and then their children's behavior...I would absolutely recommend it to friends and clients."

-Lisa Y. Pierce, MD Child and Adolescent Psychiatrist

"A great read! ...Dr. Rees has always impressed me with his easy rapport and insightful acumen... I am happy his book, Tri-C Parenting, has finally come to fruition so that it can help guide a broader population of parents who may be struggling with their children's behaviors."

-William T. Goldman, MD, DABPN Child, Adolescent & Adult Psychiatry

Tri-C Parenting

Clear. Confident. Complete.

The Fundamental Guide to Effectively Parenting Your Kid from 1st through 12th Grade

Brian Rees, PhD

I have changed some names to protect individuals' privacy.
This book does not replace the advice of a medical professional. Consult your physician or licensed therapist, before making any changes to your regular mental health plan.

Paperback ISBN: 978-1-7367584-1-0 (2nd Edition)
EBook ISBN: 978-1-7367584-0-3
Library of Congress LCCN: 2021907227

First Paperback Edition October 2021

Edited By: Stephi Cham
Illustrated & Design By: Monique Hayes

Published by Rees Core Inc.
400 N. Main St. Ste. 104, Grapevine, TX 76051

www.TriCParenting.com

DEDICATION

To my three FPE, BMJ children: Kate, Landry, and Reagan, who made Heather and me parents.

CONTENTS

Introduction........1
Let Me Set the Table........4
You........8
Clear........38
Confident........89
Complete........103
References........116
About The Author........119

Introduction

Hi everybody, welcome to Tri-C Parenting. As a mental health professional, I have treated thousands of kids and helped all types of parents for over 15 years. Looking for a complete and fundamental guide to parenting? You've come to the right place.

Based on my education and years of clinical work, my experience has shown that the parent is the number one agent of outcome in a child's life, more than any teacher, coach, or friend. I know: those are mighty powerful words. Therefore, regardless of what type of person you are, what type of kid you have, or what the world happens to be like, this approach is a method to help you parent successfully. It's a method which I've shared with countless parents and have had tremendous success.

I once heard a speaker at a childhood development conference proclaim, "There is no parenting script." And to that I say: Actually, there is.

Parents in my office consistently ask, "Do you have a book? Or something online? You make it sound so easy!" And the great thing is, that once you master this system, parenting is easy. Or maybe I should say, it's much easier. And enjoyable, to be quite honest.

You're probably reading this book for one of two reasons. Either you are having some issues with your child, or you would like some professional guidance on parenting in today's ever-changing society of maximum stress, watered-down accountability, keeping up with the Joneses, social media, compromised morals, information and technology overload, and instant gratification. *Whew!*

Fear not. This timeless model will take you to the heart of productive parenting. From math to art to nearly every sport, sustained success hinges on properly met basics.

Coaches constantly push, "Fundamentals, fundamentals, *fundamentals*!" Think of it this way. Elite athletes do not necessarily possess the exact same abilities, but through massive commitment, they all had to become foundationally solid. And once they did, not only did their game distinctively elevate, but they were able to personally customize their approach. It's the same for parenting.

Findings reviewed in 2019 from the Center for Disease Control and Prevention (CDC) report nearly one in three children suffer from some kind of mental/behavioral disorder. Allow me to make this statement which explains why I wrote this book. Whether kids are five or fifteen years old, they haven't been on the planet long enough for tons of *personal* dysfunction to build. However, in many youngsters, dysfunction appears to be present, and a major contributor is ineffective parenting.

Consistently being good parents is hard! Why? Humans, young or old, are very complex. We come from numerous backgrounds, deal with diverse social norms, can have hugely contrasting personalities and belief systems, possess different strengths and weaknesses, and can communicate and interpret information very differently. This means that in the vast realm of parenting, there's a great deal of variation. Although we all desire the same outcome—to be responsible parents who raise great kids—sound formulas consistently produce the desired results because there's hardly, if any, variation.

And when we finally became parents, most of us didn't realize what we'd actually signed up for. Holy cow the commitment is astounding. Right off the bat it's a struggle. Good thing babies are cute. Then the challenges evolve. Just when you believe it's supposed to get easier because your child is getting older, it can get harder.

But wait. There are more glaring factors that cause us to flounder. Throughout we must deal with our own individual problems, unfortunate self-centeredness, unrealistic expectations placed on our kids, and an understandable lack of patience. It's no mystery: healthy parenting must counter these humanistic defects daily, and that is almost asking the impossible. We clearly have embarked on a king-sized, unremitting assignment.

Therefore, I understand why the speaker at that conference said there is no parenting script, but that statement is misleading. The objective is to raise your new, original person successfully, but we must stay rooted in reality, which is to become the best parental version of ourselves to appropriately shape the best possible version of our child. So, no matter what society is forcing upon a kid, or what any adult or child happens to be like, if there were just one legitimate and professional approach conveyed in such a way that nearly every parent or acting parent could grasp and implement correctly, that would be awesome. A *valid guidebook,* so to speak. I know this sounds ambitious—but I've got something special I want to share with you.

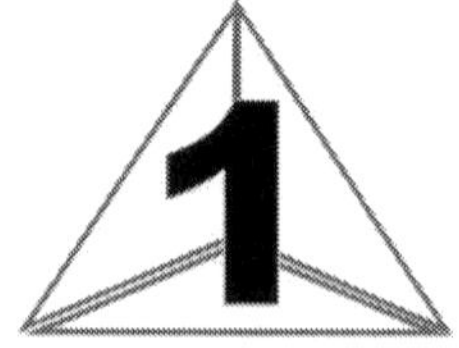

Let Me Set the Table

While absolute perfection is nonexistent, this fundamentals-heavy blueprint continues to clinically prove it can make things remarkably better, despite all the variables and challenges. It's called the **Tri-C Parenting Model**: **Clear. Confident. Complete.**

Clear – Distorted expectations are a dagger to the heart of the invaluable parent-child relationship; therefore, you will learn to look at your child through a clear, practical lens so your expectations will be accurate. You will profoundly recognize the relationship must be maintained above all else so your treasured kid will be receptive to your parenting. Your clear communication will be respectful, and you will equip your youngster to become self-responsible.

Confident – The game-changer for humans. Life is hard for all of us, but self-confident people navigate existence to the fullest. You will tirelessly instill maximum confidence in your kid(s) for all the obvious reasons. Parents are tasked to empower their children to strive and believe in themselves.

Complete – Tri-C is a complete parenting system, and you will aspire to be the appropriate parent throughout your kid's upbringing and complete important parenting tasks every day, every month, and every year. This might sound difficult, but I promise it gets increasingly easier if you can make the commitment and properly integrate my Tri-C Parenting model.

Disclaimer: This approach is designed to work for everyone and can successfully be implemented at any time, unless your child:

1. Is moderately to severely autistic.
2. Has a sub-80 IQ.
3. Was gravely abused or neglected in some capacity.
4. Has a personality disorder. (This is rare and unfixable, and it must be identified by a mental health professional.)
5. Is battling a significant problem with drugs or alcohol.
6. Has parents who plot against each other.

Also, some youngsters deal with a mental condition or two (e.g., depression, anxiety, ADHD, executive functioning deficiencies) that can cause serious issues, or some kids have completely derailed for whatever reason and the parent has lost control.

The fundamental Tri-C model is designed to teach you how to masterfully navigate parent-child concerns and raise your kid to become a rock-solid human being. This book is meant to be read front-to-back, and I kept it brief for two reasons. One, there's no need for you to be overloaded with too much information. As you progress through these pages and learn this system, you will see what I mean. And two, I want you to easily flip back through to reread sections as you see fit.

My clientele often consists of scared and frustrated parents whose kids act chronically defiant, seem unusually odd or clueless, have ADHD, dabble with drugs/vapes/alcohol, or feel depressed or anxious. Effectively raising children is hard enough, and when you throw in one or more of these problems—combined with exasperated parents—things can rapidly go downhill. I constructed this parenting philosophy to work in the most challenging of parent-child scenarios because I had to, which means that if family life already tends to go well for you, the Tri-C concepts should be easier to implement.

And, if things at home do go relatively smoothly, it's most likely because you already are a marvelous parent or you have a responsible-acting child who is genetically hard-wired to be cooperative, and who isn't grappling with any personal issues. However, some of you might be tailored to be marvelous parents but you've got a stubborn kid who is hard-wired with a strong-willed mindset (possibly paired with a mental disturbance, which can enhance difficulties). We do not get to decide how our child is engineered.

And when I say genetically hard-wired, I mean naturally predisposed, like being either right- or left-handed. In other words, children do not choose to begin their lives acting troublesome or to have mental issues. Why would they? **It is important you understand this**.

The misguided parent can worsen the problems and compel the suffering youngster to progressively become more unmanageable or symptomatic. That dark childhood road leads to feeling wretched about oneself, which spells a horrible existence. You do not want that type of avoidable outcome for your kiddo.

And for headstrong kids (which certainly does not mean they're bad kids), behavioral challenges at home can appear regularly. But when the adult learns how to correctly interact and create a functional family environment (Tri-C will show you how), things tend to joyously improve. Also, once this positive parental ball gets rolling and locked in, many negative symptoms compounded from a possible mental issue almost always subside.

That's how much power you've got.

However, if a sound Tri-C baseline has been established for a few months and serious problems continue, outside help is most likely necessary. The first choice would be to locate a mental health professional who treats children, but if that's not a viable option, then some type of formal clinic or program for kids in your community that's run by devoted adults. Still, remember to firmly maintain Tri-C throughout and after any type of involvement from outside the home, as the fundamental principles of this model are widely applicable and timeless.

You

Let's look at what type of parent you are and go from there. Not getting to actually meet you and talk to your child creates some hurdles, but I'll do my best within these pages to teach you this philosophy.

Regarding the style of how I chose to write this book: I don't believe I can accurately express Tri-C with a bunch of sugarcoating, and there's nothing sexy about great parenting. Parents in my office tell me they appreciate my straightforward manner, so I'll use that same approach here. I'm going to communicate with you as if we've already developed some trust and you're cool with me speaking very openly. And because I unfortunately don't have the luxury of getting to have personal conversations with you, and these printed words are all I've got, some of the phraseology I use might come across as a little strong—please understand that I'm merely trying to make or drive home an important point.

Something else to note: you're going to see some repetition. Why? To recalibrate certain hardened areas of the brain is no small task. I've had super sharp parents in my office repeatedly to the point where it feels like Groundhog Day so we can revisit some of these concepts. But once the dedicated adults get it (just like when things "click" for fully committed athletes), it's wonderful. I also encourage spouses and significant others to read this book together, especially during the early phases of implementing Tri-C, to help coach each other and understand this process.

In a classic system (which some of you may recognize) developed by Diana Baumrind, parenting styles can generally be categorized as Permissive, Authoritarian, Neglectful, and Authoritative. I've added one called "Compassionate Boss" because I encounter a bunch of these folks in my office. Listed below are modified descriptions of each, so let's determine what your tendencies might be as you should fall into one of these categories.

Permissive - You're more of a friend than of a parent. You certainly love and want the best for your child, but you tend to *enable*. You hesitate to enforce age-appropriate rules, easily cave in, and dislike conflict. Example: You allow your kid too much time playing video games to avoid potential confrontation and because you want your child to "be happy."

Authoritarian - You are in charge! You love and want the best for your kid, but you tend to harshly punish for not meeting your requirements and you are always right. You provide direction *ad nauseam*, deeply enforce your personal agenda, and communicate however you want. The authoritarian tends to disregard the mighty value of the parent-child union.

Neglectful - Uninvolved. Disconnected. Selfish. Immature. This excuse-making parent provides little support if any, and typically does not read books like this.

Authoritative - Vastly different than Authoritarian, although you are the captain. You unabashedly love, respect, and prize your child. You set age-appropriate, reasonable rules. You empower and do not enable. Your consequences and rewards are fair and consistent. You teach self-responsibility and avoid lectures. You strongly honor the parent-child relationship, encourage cooperation, maintain relatability, and instill confidence and the emotional support necessary for your kid to create healthy goals.

Compassionate Boss - You demonstrate many of the same positive characteristics as Authoritative, although you tend to communicate in a more straightforward, demanding style as you blend in a little Authoritarian force. Easygoing kids can mostly tolerate this approach because they see the big picture and understand your abruptness is wrapped in goodness and love. However, strong-willed children are more black-and-white thinkers. They often fail to see the big picture, want what they want, wrestle with change, and struggle to read between the lines (i.e., they often misinterpret meanings and regularly take things too personally). Therefore, a compassionate boss–willful child combo can routinely experience problems.

Undoubtedly, Authoritative sounds best, and my guess is most of you try to parent this way, want to parent this way, or at some point tried to parent this way but somehow got derailed. I am a realist, so I understand I cannot change your personality, nor do I want to, and I think it's fantastic you're taking your valuable time to read this. But if you fall more into the Permissive, Authoritarian, or Compassionate Boss types, you will be asked to consider permanently adjusting some aspects of communication with your kid.

As you begin to administer Tri-C, it can be uncomfortable to alter an old, locked-in parenting tendency that might sometimes work, or may have worked when your child was much younger. You're reading this book because you possess a strong desire to better understand your kid and to be a great parent, and in the deep crevasses of your mind, especially when your old habits are screaming at you to return to your prior, ineffective ways, you know you must devote yourself to a new method.

Productive parenting awaits.

Lesson One: Respect

Lesson One is to help you understand some things about yourself and your child, create some new thinking, and place value on consistent, respectful interaction.

Let's look at what arguably is the *numero uno* trademark that bluntly sabotages respectfulness, then work on fixing it. This common flaw is based on a detrimental adult belief that states we know how our kid is *supposed* to act, and how we parents *should get to* act. As the authority figure in the parent-child arrangement, the age-old doctrine goes something like this:

I'm the adult, you're the child; I can say whatever I want and treat you however I want, and I should expect you to meet all reasonable expectations.

Of the three parts of this notion, the first and last parts are accurate.

I am the adult, you're the child.

Correct.

I should expect you to meet all reasonable expectations. Correct.

However, there's a twist concerning the middle section: *I can say whatever I want and treat you however I want.*

Hold up.

When our child is choosing to not meet an expectation (e.g., "Get off your phone." "Quit sneaking food in your bedroom." "Stop hitting your brother!") and we're becoming frustrated, it's easy to communicate abrasively. Sometimes we seem to discount the fact that our child is a real person, and we treat that young human with zero consideration. (We are all guilty of this.) Permanently fixing this negative behavior is extremely difficult, but must be carried out. That is why I have placed "staying respectful" as the first big issue to address. You might be thinking *Hmm. Of all the parenting topics he could've opened with, he chose this.*

Yes I did.

Regardless of whether we're the parent, stepparent, single parent, foster parent, or family member raising the kid(s), we have two Primary Parental Tasks:

- Appropriately protect our children
- Appropriately develop our children

Everything falls under these two umbrellas. Therefore, we must communicate in a style with which our kids fully trust us and are accepting of what we say. If we can't effectively communicate and our kids do not embrace our guidance, then we fail to meet the two tasks, and good parenting becomes futile. Our children must mind us so we can keep them safe, and our kids must *want* to listen to us so we can prepare them to become high-functioning adults. We have to earn credibility with our kids. (Yes, I said we adults have to earn it, not demand it.)

So why can parents act like such donkeys' rears to their child—the individual cherished above all things in the universe? Because we are people. And when our kid isn't listening, or is being disagreeable, or is making a dumb decision, or maybe we're just having a bad day, we potentially fall into the habit of believing *I can say whatever I want and treat you however I want.*

A frustrated mom and her adolescent son were in my office getting into it. I was nearly begging her to stop being inflammatory and to recognize that her harmful interaction towards him was completely messing up the goal, which was to productively discuss why he was doing badly in two of his classes. As soon as her "parental tone" got more challenging, his willful mind (a mind that has a hard time seeing the big picture) compelled him to get defensive and a bit disrespectful. Instead of choosing to take just a second and acknowledge her child's naturally ornery personality (which would help her raise potentially provoking topics in a way that would keep him rational), she quickly did what many parents would do: she gave in to anger and grabbed the "gas can." *Ka-boom! Argument explosion!*

Constructive conversation over. Credibility deterioration. She allowed her frustration to dominate her thinking and behavior. *I'm the parent! Do not argue with me!*

The mom and I kept working together for a while, and once this parent learned to automatically activate Tri-C guidelines in these types of situations (like you will), no more explosions occurred. Because their relationship had gotten behind the 8 ball, she, being *the adult,* was responsible for luring him back to a place of positivity. And eventually, she did! Victory! No more hyped frustration, no more fighting, no more back-and-forth disrespect.

The young child who had grown into a teenager finally liked and trusted his mom again, and was much more receptive to promptly meeting responsibilities. She abandoned her old, inaccurate thinking and embraced a new, correct mindset. She put in the work, and her kid naturally followed.

When earlier I mentioned that children tend to inherently be more cooperative or more rigid-minded, let me add, this personality characteristic is on a continuum. Again, some kids are hardwired to be super agreeable, some are wired to be super inflexible, and the rest fall somewhere in between, and our kids' genetic disposition tends to influence how we treat them. Hence, stubborn children make it more difficult for us to stay respectful.

Dr. James Dobson, author of the highly touted book, *The Strong-Willed Child,* warns that parenting a tougher kid can lead us to become a screamer and/or a tyrant, as that young person constantly pushes back (that is, until Tri-C becomes the existing norm) and makes it incredibly challenging to find the balance between love and control.

I had a frustrated dad in my office discussing his oldest son. He asked, “Do you treat any strong-willed kids?” My first thought was *If I had a nickel...*

But I answered, “If I see fifty kids a week, thirty are in here because they’re strong-willed.”

“Well, my kid seems to act defiant just to be defiant. When I tell him to do something, he’ll actually cop an attitude and ask me why. Can you believe that?”

“What do you say?” I asked.

He huffed, “’Because I freaking said so.’ That’s what I say.”

I winced a little. “And how does that go?”

“Well lately, pretty badly.” He paused. “Now that I’m thinking about it, I don’t think that kid can stand me.”

I appreciated this father having enough awareness to see that his child didn’t like him, and sadly, why would he? This dad certainly had likable traits, but every day he was acting more and more like a jerk as he tried to force respect.

That never works.

Now listen, some of you may be thinking, *My kid has to respect me—I’m the parent.* Here’s where we begin some mental recalibration. If we’re going to get real, then no, your child does not have to respect you.

What I’m about to reiterate is very important to comprehend and is addressed throughout the book: For naturally easygoing children, negative interactions with their folks are minimal because mindful, emotionally mature kids understand their parents and recognize it’s in their best interest to act respectful. Because they “get it,” they’re in the business of keeping the peace, not flipping over the apple cart. We can essentially parent these kids however we want and they will mind us.

However, humans are not automatons. That is why a fair

amount of this manual addresses how to effectively parent youngsters who do not want to consistently mind. As a matter of fact, I'm not so sure there would be any parenting books past the toddler years if every kid mechanically minded.

With that being said, there are parents who must raise intrinsically iron-willed children, and lots of these kids arrive on Planet Earth. They tend to have tunnel vision and getting what they want (or being right, or having the last word) appears to be the most important thing. Because they can be short on empathy (i.e., placing value on other's wants and feelings, especially if it doesn't align with their own), big problems with their folks regularly emerge. Baffled parents in my office of these types of children will ask, "Wait a minute, you mean my kid was born like this?"

I'll nod, "That is correct."

Unfortunately, a headstrong kid and parent can become at serious odds as the child actually loses "obligated" respect for the now forceful adult. The incited youngster will regularly begin to defy, manipulate, lie, and argue, feeling more discouraged and try to fight with or wear down the caregiver—either passively or aggressively—to determine what the frazzled parent will allow because "Why the heck not? I don't like you and you make my life worse anyway, and I don't possess the recognition to grasp the fact that if I stopped provoking you and acted more agreeably, you would be nicer to me." This immature mindset fosters lots of back-and-forth disrespectful interaction. Down, down, down you go.

Believe it or not, your child knows who the big cheese is. If you have a stubborn kid (ranging anywhere from mild to severe on the hard-headedness scale) who evolves into not liking you*? Forget about it.* The relationship will grow into a "me versus you" dynamic. I assume a decent number of you readers, regrettably, can somewhat identify with this, and you did not intend for your life as a parent to heartbreakingly unroll like that. If this quandary sounds familiar, know this book is designed to teach you a selection of fundamental concepts (whether you've got a strong-willed kid or not) which include how to successfully satisfy these two important questions:

1. Can I, the adult in the driver's seat, maintain a high level of overall maturity and awareness when dealing with my kid, anywhere and in any capacity?

2. Can I, the adult, consistently execute an effective method of communication in such a way that my child will *want* to comply with my parenting year after year, anywhere and in any capacity?

Here's a standard example of a parent who did not do the above. Some of you probably have witnessed something similar. I saw a hardened mom screaming in public at her six- or seven-year-old son who was behaving like a spirited youngster with lots of energy.

"What's wrong with you?" she screeched. "You need to listen to me! Get over here!" She then grabbed him by the arm and got in his face for a few more choice words as he scowled and tried to pull away. We have a decent idea of that mom's twisted thinking:

1. I'm in charge. I can treat you with zero respect, especially if you've upset or scared me in some way.

2. How dare you continue to defy me! You make me treat you like this!

3. Everyone witnessing this needs to know I'm powerful and in control, and the best way to show that is to be fearsome!

What in the world was she trying to accomplish? Where was she going with that? *(Lest we forget, one day that child will become a teenager...)*

I've had headstrong children in my office break down and cry because they feel tremendous, internal conflict as they struggle to be less obstinate, but aren't yet developed enough to mitigate that personality trait. As mentioned earlier, this is the most common issue I treat: kids who tend to be hardheaded and don't know how to handle a significant number of life challenges, including how to get along with their parents. Navigating childhood and adolescence is hard enough for young people these days, even the ones who mostly comprehend what is happening around them.

For inherently rigid kids, their parents' job is to recognize that particular hardwiring and not make things worse. These parents must (keyword: must) make things better by being the champions who help productively advance these "tough to raise" individuals into pleasant, yet strong adults with high self-confidence, determination, and a decent sense of empathy for others. Maintaining a positive relationship throughout upbringing can take enormous work, as many of these unnerved parents report they seem to spend all their time trying to deal with their kids' oblivion which gets exhausting. And this "oblivion" can evolve into all kinds of negative personal and social issues when they become adults, which is why it is so important to parent them correctly while they're young.

And, not uncommonly, parents with a stubborn child can get tricked. Their kid can have beautiful, random moments of total clarity. Unlike with Forrest Gump, who reminded us at every turn he had "issues," parents of a willful child often think, *My kid does get it! I actually can relax and communicate however I want!* Guess again.

Consider this. You're a human, and your child is a human, and human beings "want what they want" and generally have the means to acquire it. That's why we rule the planet. You are an adult who has learned that if what you desire is not what the establishment allows, then you will suffer a consequence if you resist or get caught. Through years of experience you've made the proper adjustments.

Children do not have that luxury. They are not experienced people but still powerful entities: naturally moody, feeling overruled, yet vigorously testing the world around them. This is very normal (you did it). Keep this in mind when you're being challenged by your youngsters, as most parents fall into the trap of getting angry too easily or taking what their kids say or do personally.

The more we're able to look at our kid (and sometimes ourselves) realistically, the more our expectations become accurate for our child, and, in certain situations, for us parents too. Lots of parents, mostly moms, get caught up in allowing their child to hurt their feelings, as mothers unfortunately tend to be regarded as the readily available, soft target. When humans feel emotionally hurt, we tend to respond negatively. Although all of us parents are (ahem) mature, we are still people, sometimes completely drained, impatient, and vexed by disrespect—all parent-child relationship wrecking balls.

Well guess what? A child or teenager is just a goofy kid who you will learn doesn't have any emotional power over you when it comes to hurting your feelings or making you mad. *None.* We will revisit this concept throughout the book because it is such a parenting handicap. **Harsh, knee-jerk parental responses triggered by our anger/fear/hurt are bad and immediately throw a wrench in the entire process before we can even begin.** In other words, when your child is being unruly, *do not take that kid seriously.* I cannot overemphasize this enough. Your diligent, Tri-C application will ultimately motivate your child to not want to defy you.

I've also treated way too many kids who complain that their parents generally don't seem to care who they are, what they think, or how they feel (which is awful to hear). They tell me their folks treat them with zero courtesy as they just mindlessly bark orders all the time. More fortunate children tell me they feel encouraged to be respectful because their parents are consistently respectful towards them. They see how some other parents treat their kids inconsiderately, and they appreciate the continuous efforts their own parents' model to stay understanding.

> Know this: A child will follow a parent's lead because you are the leader. You set the tone of the relationships in the household: either more upbeat, dignified, and respectful, or more negative, chaotic, and disconnected. If things are bad and you need to reset the tone, you can. This can be difficult at first, but not impossible. Do not let up. Stay with Tri-C.

Now, back to the frustrated dad in my office. Once this loving yet distressed father was able to accept he had a naturally willful child, he realized he would need to be the one to change instead of expecting his kid to supernaturally change. He was able to shift his focus to what was more important. Rather than intensely and hopelessly clutching the perspective of "I'm the parent! You will do what I say!" he finally came to understand this:

The most important thing is for my kid to be *receptive to my parenting*, and that is on me. I must alter my inaccurate, predetermined mindset and understand it will be easier for me to modify how I communicate than for my son to change how he interprets information. Because if I don't, then what? My kid won't ever learn from me all the things I'm supposed to teach him? We will fight constantly? Disastrous!

Hence, a large part of the first "C" of the Tri-C Model, *clear* expectations, promotes respectful dialogue. This motivates the child to be more agreeable and allows us parents to better give our attention to honoring the relationship instead of giving in to reactionary selfishness, adult entitlement, and negative thoughts towards our very own (or adopted) flesh and blood. Feeling negative about your own child stinks and is unacceptable.

I've seen numerous parents who've become so disenchanted with their kid that most interactions have become horrid and any remnants of good parenting are gone. Their ongoing anger towards their child prompts them to hastily throw kerosene on the flame instead of utilizing their power to fix things. It's tragic.

Allow me to restate an important truth that will help you stay respectful, even when your kid is acting mouthy or irresponsible. Everyone knows who is ultimately in charge: you. The parent. You have the ability to make your kid's life wonderful or dreadful, and all parties know this. You have all the authority and you child has none. You do not have to argue in any fashion about who has the power. Try your hardest to not get overly upset when your kid chooses to be sassy or disagreeable. Every time you respond negatively, you poison your parenting and take three steps back.

Poison my parenting? Three steps back? From what? From persuading your kid to like and respect you. You must continuously build your case year after year for that person to *want* to do as you say, not *have* to do what you say; there is a huge difference. Your kiddo cannot afford for you to get lazy, discouraged, disconnected, or to regularly be mad or you will lose that child.

Raising a human is unquestionably the most valuable thing you will ever engage in as you commit to the long game of parenting. You've been personally tasked to help a young individual become healthy on the inside and out, and get to adulthood feeling as self-assured as possible. If you were in my office and I figured you parented either more dictatorially or dismissively, we might explore that and try to understand why you felt the need to be that way. And during this conversation, if you were open to embracing what Tri-C is all about, my hopeful assumption would be that you are willing to dedicate yourself to doing what needs to be done to become an amazing parent for your kid. I will not mislead you and advertise that great parenting is a walk in the park, but I will reiterate that the Tri-C system, implemented faithfully, makes parenting exponentially easier and more gratifying. You win and your kid wins. But as you know, in order to win most things, serious effort has to be put forth.

What I will stress throughout this entire book is for you to instantaneously recognize how you are communicating with your child, no matter the circumstance and no matter the youngster's personality, and choose to engage the right way—the Tri-C way—because it is *worth it*. In other words, you will no longer just voice things and act however you want, think it's fine, and expect your youngster to brainlessly follow your direction; you will learn how to steadily interact correctly so your kid will consistently accept your parenting and *thrive* from meeting your direction.

Sometimes adults seem to forget their child is not some pawn to arrogantly move around as they see fit—the kid is a real person, the most invaluable investment ever and a direct representation of the parents. A byproduct, so to speak, whose outcome is crucially and indisputably shaped by the caregivers' eighteen-year style of child management. A human's initial exposure to life takes place during childhood and adolescence, so if said human is given the strength and opportunity to navigate the early years boldly and successfully, chances are strong that particular individual will be equipped to also successfully manage the long remainder of adult life.

And do not think for one second Tri-C is about being a pushover or me asking you to wear kid gloves; this warm, science-based system is about effective parenting, period. Let's keep going.

Lesson Two: Relationship Design

Lesson Two focuses on the most powerful, fundamental dimension of productive parenting: the formation of the parent-child relationship.

This doctrine cannot be dismissed in any fashion, for two reasons:

1. **A positive relationship is the lynchpin of parenting successfully.**
2. **A negative relationship is the mighty downfall.**

Therefore, if our relationship with someone is good (and we all desire healthy human connections, especially with our folks), we're motivated to keep it that way because we like the person and want to be liked in return. But what about our feelings and behavior towards someone we do not like? *That looks much different.* We don't care what that person wants or how the person feels, and it doesn't matter whom we're talking about. So if the parent chooses not to be consistently respectful towards the child, not only is the high-ranking adult setting a horrible example as a kid tends to mirror the caregiver's behavior, why would the kid care about the parent or what the parent says?

Think of it like this: although we wear a few different hats with our children, we essentially are "the boss." During our own working careers, most of us have had a good boss and a bad boss. The good supervisor you genuinely *like*. You're not necessarily going out after work, but because of how graciously you're treated on a consistent basis, you honor the relationship with utmost respect. You're cool with working hard and meeting the demands of the job, and a big reason is because of your positive feelings towards that person.

But the bad boss who acts disrespectfully, critically, and/or dismissively towards you creates an entirely different feeling. You honestly can't stand that bozo and DO NOT CARE what that jerk wants, and the only reason you act dutiful is because you need a paycheck. Yuck. Whether you like it or not, *you will* create a version of one of these two dynamics at home.

There are two different ways to style the relationship with your kid. One manner is the Directive Way. The parent rigidly focuses the majority of attention only on what the child is or isn't doing, and places erratic, unfair conditions on when to demonstrate love, respect, and approval.

The second is the Connected Way. This also involves responding to the child's behavior, but the mature, confident parent consistently demonstrates monumental interest in who the kid is (which does not include enabling, by the way). These dramatically different practices will create two very different brands of relationships.

It's natural for many parents to submerge into the faulty first method. As a parent, *if I must protect and develop you, I must unduly focus on your actions* (especially at the onset of child-rearing when that little rascal likes to run through the parking lot and sling oatmeal all over the kitchen and whack the TV with a plastic bat). Which brings us back to excessive demonstrations of *I'm the parent, you're the child, and you will do what I say.*

An early custom of significant control becomes established. The practice of "do what I tell you" has to work because it's exhausting trying to reason with a three-year-old. But that small child quickly grows into a six-year-old who can be more reasonable and "talked with" instead of "talked at." No one likes to be talked at, by the way. And for that matter, nobody likes to be controlled or told what to do or how to be, and this includes your human child (which I'm sure you've noticed).

So if we're going to be honest, the commanding "Do what I say because I'm more concerned with controlling your behavior than treating you with consideration" practice is an easier way to parent. Also, it alludes to the dismissive, yet accepted philosophy of "I say jump, you say how high." Again, this relationship-crushing, disrespectful approach is so commonplace and so regularly executed that it might be fair to say it's the number one administered killer of good parenting. (Shame and guilt are two and three, and many parents don't even consciously realize when they're doing it.)

What's even worse is that not only is this lazy parenting, for many adults, it also feels good to be powerful—inappropriately, unnecessarily powerful. I know that sounds terrible, but it's true. It's almost as if they finally have somebody they can boss around and treat however they want. If you haven't already, look into the research project *The Stanford Prison Experiment* and you will see what I mean.

Another factor which fuels a controlling, disconnected relationship is that grown-ups and children, blood or not, do not have a ton in common. We don't see non-family adults and kids just hanging out for the heck of it. Plus, your job is to be responsible for the well-being of your children, not to be their friend (until they are grown). It's almost paradoxical to be friendly and not be a friend.

But wait. The most pivotal component of good parenting is *for my children to like and respect me so they will be more responsive to all that I communicate, from how much I love you, to eat your green beans, to getting high is not permitted.* Kids are humans (not dogs), and once more, people hate to be controlled.

Okay Brian, then what you're saying is, I must work to find the sweet spot throughout my child's entire upbringing? The sweet spot between managing my kid (which must include control) and consistently demonstrating an unwavering, respectful message that I'm unquestionably interested in who this young person actually is?

Correct. This is your objective, especially as your child gets older and grows in awareness. And as you dedicate yourself to respectful interaction and execute the Tri-C principles, the parenting sweet spot becomes much larger and easier to hit.

Which brings us back to the Connected Way: You clearly are as interested in who the child is as you are in any behavior that's being demonstrated. Because if you express constant, meaningful regard, that must certainly indicate how much respect you have for your kid as *a person*. There is no such thing as a healthy relationship without everlasting respect. I find myself saying to intimidating parents who try to dominate, "Your child should never fear you—only the consequences you can impose."

As adults, we have learned to convey what we're trying to communicate to other adults respectfully; otherwise, we would have zero friends and zero credibility with others. Therefore, we must maintain this principle when interacting with our child. In other words, the same rules of receptive communication apply. I also tell parents regularly, "You're very likable and you know how to get people to like you; get your kid to like you." So once the connected relationship theme is established (because we've learned to get over ourselves) and the youngster knows the parent is committed to it, a few prime elements are addressed.

One, your child feels accepted by the all-important caregiver, which escorts your young individual down a developmentally healthy path of life. This path is different than the destructive path created by the critical, detached, or overly controlling parent. That road leads to doom.

The world is a big, scary place for a child, and your appropriate interaction at every turn gives your kid the reassurance to feel secure, which fosters more "normal" functioning. Normal functioning leads to easier parenting, and I think it's safe to say we are all into easier parenting.

The kid feels loved, safe, and accepted, and can primarily focus on bold steps to consistently move forward. What is not good is your child dealing with assorted or steady disapproval, and all the dreadful elements attached to that nonsense. Insecurity: *Baaaaaaaad.* The differences between a child with devoted parents versus a child with forceful, enabling, or disconnected parents can be astounding.

Emotionally deprived or beat-down kids become full of self-doubt and can feel like they don't have much to live for. Thus, they can make a lifetime of frightful decisions just to personally or socially feel better, or self-victimize, or cower, or demonstrate (something I also see with entitled kids) glaring defiance. On the other hand, children who are richly parented and invested in life have a lot to lose and feel empowered to achieve success. These kids develop a healthy ambition and don't want anything to potentially mess that up. They know the mom and/or dad have the means to sabotage a desired way of life if bad choices are made.

Plainly stated, the Tri-C fostered Connected Way relationship energizes your kid to want to mind you. *Want.* And now that you've clearly forged an eternal bond due to your patience, understanding, and fabulousness, your child grows in confidence, accepts your leadership, seeks your approval, and becomes more inclined to continuously meet real-world standards you set forth. Nice!

And the closer you are in your relationship, the easier it will be for you to understand how your child communicates and interprets information, which helps you find the correct broadband to transmit on. Plus, you'll more easily detect personal struggles throughout upbringing. Have no doubt: there will be difficulties, and that applies to all young people.

You'll be *trusted*, and able to have open conversations and provide vital support when needed. For example, if some legitimate depression has crept into your child's life, you must be able to see that and appropriately address it. Regarding all childhood issues, you're expected to properly assist your kid and help that neophyte learn how to figure out life (assist, not rescue or take over). You have the know-how; your kid does not.

Parent-Teen Connection: Teenagers can make it especially difficult to stay bonded. Adolescents are gradually and naturally separating themselves from their parents, which allows them to develop their own identities and get ready for upcoming independence. Due to this normal phase of uncoupling, these soon-to-be young adults' short-lived lack of interest in their folks makes it tough to chat about personal and recreational things, leaving us parents feeling forced to talk only about upholding responsibilities. These administrative or instructional discussions are also known as... "lectures."

It's hard for some of us parents to have been so wonderfully connected with our child for twelve or thirteen years, then all of a sudden, *The kid doesn't much seem to give a flip about me.* Accept this teenage developmental reality and vigorously uphold your position by being connected, not directive. Regardless of how much or how little time you're spending together, make sure to stay respectful and try to focus conversations on non-administrative subjects when you can; otherwise, your teenager will want to disconnect even more.

I've heard plenty of parents lament the decline of the bond with their aging teen, so remember: the process of reconnecting in adulthood (where the two of you will spend the majority of your time together—as two adults, which sounds crazy, I know) is strengthened if you kept it cool all throughout your child's adolescence. Plus, the more understanding you are during the later child-rearing years, the more credibility you'll have, and the more your teenager will want to be with and listen to you.

I was working with a stubborn teenage girl and her mom (the apple hadn't fallen far from the tree). I asked the daughter how much she felt like the discussions with her parents were administrative.

She wrinkled her nose and said, "About 80 percent." After her mother stepped out, the adolescent frowned. "It's more like 95 percent."

When I had them switch places, the mother tried to defend the 80% remark: "It's because she won't do what we say."

I hear that a lot. That's why this book contains specific ways to inspire your kid to meet your requirements. But know this: you will have to fully receive the Tri-C philosophy—as this is not merely about executing pedestrian techniques—and follow its deep essence to the letter, or there's a strong possibility it will not work.

While we're on the subject of teenagers—because those people are at the age where they mostly know what they should (and should not) be doing—realize that it's beneficial for the parent to do more of the listening instead of the talking. You've probably heard this before because it's true. For some of us this is another important mental recalibration, but a listening approach allows kids the opportunity to work out their own problems, develop healthy coping mechanisms, and put together self-directed answers. So when you catch yourself droning on and on, *stop*.

Try to recognize what you're negatively doing and understand you are serving your own anxiety or agenda, not your child's development. If your kid is shutting down, you are not communicating your point effectively. *Take a breath*. Then, either let it go and trust the fact you'll have an opportunity to revisit it, or reshape that monologue into a shared discussion so your kid will want to listen to what you have to say.

As parents, we've certainly got experienced opinions we feel are necessary to convey. But what I'm saying is, there are effective ways to express our wise messages. I can't begin to tell you how many parents I've had in my office who continue to lecture, even after we've discussed its ineffectiveness. Maybe they just love to hear the sound of their own voice.

In the mom-daughter scenario described above, the dad came to the session the following week. He was a nice enough guy, but he continued to bang his head against the wall as he fixated on telling his daughter what the expectations were, rather than recognizing his communication style wasn't working. (What's that well-known definition of insanity?) He was all about what *he wanted*, also known as the Directive Way.

His pompous approach demonstrated it was more important to

him to lazily dismiss his daughter's natural shortcomings in awareness, and disrespectfully just "tell her what to do" rather than to mentally reconfigure his parental thinking and take into account what was especially critical: for him to interact in such a way that she would be responsive to him. And because his sole, hard focus was on his daughter meeting his requirements (instead of *on her),* there was no personal connection. She didn't care what he wanted, nor had she even been asked what was wrong in the first place!

In the parents' defense, this teenager wasn't very easy to bond with. Why? She wasn't overly warm and fuzzy (not her basic personality, yet she was likable enough), but also, parents tend to connect more easily with a child who consistently minds. (We appreciate that!) Plus, a kid who "gets it" tends to be more likable in the first place. As mentioned earlier, parents of a naturally strong-willed child must recognize that and know there will be steady, extra work involved to sustain a positive relationship. Sometimes it takes Herculean understanding and work, as in, *I get how you're hard-wired; therefore, I unquestionably have to keep that in mind and honor the correct way to communicate with you, especially when you're being immature or naturally uncooperative.* Otherwise, no relationship. No relationship means no genuine credibility, and no parental credibility equals defiance and misery.

And here's something else that creates some disconnect in the parent-child relationship and is a hard habit to break for some of us. Unfortunately I see parents do this all the time. Remember when I stated that when we become parents it's no longer about us? Well, your child doesn't much care and doesn't need to hear any "walking five miles in the snow" stories about your own trials growing up. (Unless you're asked, which is fun. You occasionally will be, so wait for it.)

A good principle to follow: instead of trying to provide a firsthand account about yourself to give a life lesson or make a parenting point, respectfully ask what your kid would like to do to effectively address the situation. This is big. If you can eliminate (or at least minimize) this common parenting mistake, teamed with having some patience, you'll hopefully create a conversation instead of a sermon as the two of you solve the issue together. Again, the kid (not you) needs to be the one doing most of the talking to take responsibility and work on creating solutions.

However, some of the adolescents I treat do not know exactly what they're supposed to be doing, or better yet, how to convince their parents to feel more comfortable giving them what they really want: freedom. *Freedom, freedom, freedom.* I tell these somewhat rigid-minded teenagers they are choosing not to follow a formula that works. Here's an example from a session with a struggling fifteen-year-old:

Kid: My parents aren't letting me do anything.
Me: What do you mean?
Kid: My curfew is earlier than all my friends, my mom always has to know where I am every second, I never get to do what I want, and they took away Snapchat forever. (Teens love to speak in absolutes, and everything is a big deal.)
Me: Well that's a bummer. It sounds like they don't trust you.
Kid: They don't.
Me: Why do you think that is?
Kid: I don't know. Maybe because I'm failing a couple of classes right now? And they caught me vaping last week.
Me: Yeah, that would do it.
Kid: It stinks.
Me: Hey, let me ask you this. Are their overall expectations mostly fair for a fifteen-year-old? For parents who are trying to be responsible.
Kid: I guess.
Me: And do you know what their rules are?

Kid: I think so.

Me: It sounds like they don't trust you because you're not meeting their expectations.

Kid: Well, maybe. They also nag me about doing chores.

Me: Hmm. Maybe we should look at what's more important to you.

This discouraged kid's thinking was a bit immature, in many ways closer to an eleven-year-old's (I see this a lot with hard-headed and ADHD kids: their emotional maturity doesn't always match their age, which can clearly cause problems), and his stubbornness was not helping. Instead of "giving in" to his parents, he was becoming more defiant, making the parents angrier. If this sounds familiar, you can take the lead and help your child mentally reconfigure a successful way to take some responsibility and help fix this.

It begins with a conversation, not a lecture; otherwise you would almost immediately be shut out. And if you have already launched into the Connected Way relationship, this process will be much easier.

First, calmly discuss your kid's behavior, do not express your anger, and respectfully ask *why* (we'll deeply discuss this Tri-C application in the following pages) your teen is choosing not to meet the requirement(s). State you're not in the business of being controlling; you simply need to establish trust. The more the parent trusts the kid, the more freedom is granted. *That is the formula.* A youngster earns trust by being mature and responsible, which means meeting a parent's reasonable expectations.

Me: It looks like you're more focused on doing what you want than on having more freedom.

Kid: Huh?

(I expected that reply, especially from an inflexible thinker.)

Me: Well, you tell me that what you really want is as much freedom as possible.
Kid: Yeah.
Me: Your parents decide what you get to do, and everything goes through them, right?
Kid: I guess.
Me: So the more your parents trust you, the more they'll allow you to do what you want.
Kid: I suppose.
Me: That's the formula. If you choose to meet their conditions, your parents will be impressed and trust you more. And the more they trust you, the more overall freedom you earn. They will see you making good choices, and trust that you will make good choices outside the home.
Kid: Part of my brain tells me just to do what they say, but the other half tells me, "Forget them." I don't really like them right now.
Me: Yeah, I see that. It's tough to feel negative towards your own folks.
Kid, sighing: So what should I do?
Me: That's up to you. You tell me you want freedom, so how do you think you can do a better job earning their trust? (Give the kid the responsibility where you can. Again, this is a Tri-C, front-line principle.)
Kid: Try harder in school?
Me: What else?
Kid: Don't vape? Do my chores?
Me, nodding: I promise your folks have better things to do than micro-manage you.
Kid mildly scoffs: So you mean I should just do everything they say.
Me: I'm not telling you what to do, but it looks like you've got two options.

Kid: Huh?

Me: You can either start trying to meet their expectations, or keep it going like it is.

Kid: Hmm...

Me: And I don't care which one you pick. I just know that when kids find the balance between doing what they want and taking care of their responsibilities (i.e., blending their own world and the real world—some kids are naturally good at this; some kids are not), parents act more positively towards them.

Kid sighs: I need to get better at that. I seem to have a hard time not getting my way. (We devoted some time in our sessions to helping him expand his overall perspective, and see the value in being more cooperative.)

Me: Let's say all of a sudden you do get better at it and become a responsible-acting teenager. How do you think that would go?

Kid: Man, I tried that before. Nothing changed.

Me: For how long?

Kid: I don't know. Maybe a week.

Me: I know a week to you probably seems like a long time, but to an adult it's nothing. Do you want to try an experiment?

Kid: What do you mean?

Me: Today is the 12th. Until the end of the month, let's say you legitimately try to meet their expectations the best you can, and see how they start treating you. (A literal-thinking individual does much better with concrete dialogue, dates, expressions, etc. If the kid is a black-and-white thinker, try to communicate in black-and-white terms whenever necessary. I'm serious about this. That person has trouble seeing the gray, so don't expect the kid to just "get" or accept what you're trying to say.) And if your parents are trying...

Kid: I think I can do that.

Me: If you actually pull it off? Watch the magic.

The mom came back into the session and we explained what was discussed. She seemed doubtful (she recognized he had some shortcomings in maturity, which I assured her would eventually develop and catch up in his 20s), but she agreed to do her part and be clear and respectful (i.e., watch her delivery) throughout this exercise. I explained they both wanted the same thing: for him to earn freedom through her trust. Once their parent-child perspective began to switch from "me vs. you" to a feeling of "we're in the same corner," not only did the adolescent begin to see the value of meeting his parents' expectations (and it took more than a few weeks to fully come to fruition, but we certainly got the ball rolling), this kid also realized how great it was when his parent(s) felt favorable towards him, and vice versa.

After another week had passed, they came back to the office.

"You guys are smiling," I said. "How's the experiment going?

Magic indeed.

Fear: Aside from the dysfunctional, inappropriate parents who create giant problems for their children, most adults with kids sincerely desire to be great caregivers. The most common factor that compromises good parenting (not caused by a mule-headed child who makes us want to pull out our hair) is the powerful beast known as fear. Fear often shows up as control, meaning fearful parents tend to manifest in one of two ways:

1. Helicopter or lawnmower parents who inappropriately enable or protect the youngster from ordinary life challenges.

2. Insecure, over-involved parents whose distorted senses of worth are somehow tied to the child's achievement. They fear if the kid doesn't do almost everything the parents' way then success will not be achieved, or control will be lost, or the kid will bring some degree of shame upon the parent or

family.

These ill-advised approaches cripple most of what we're trying to accomplish: to raise a confident individual. We adults know it's critical for a child to experience natural failures as the result of poor decision making or lack of effort, as areas of essential growth are fostered from misfires. So when we over-control as parents, we are interacting disrespectfully. We inhibit the youngster's growth and go against an important parental objective: to help advance self-confidence. The child is not allowed to take sufficient ownership of personal decision-making and figure out enough things independently.

Many parents in my office have admitted their anxiety consistently gets the best of them, and they know they control or coddle their child too much, but they don't know what to do about it. But have no fear (*ha*)!

Tri-C helps offset excessive policing, enabling, and disappointment by teaching the parent to interact accurately. The more we respond to our kid the right way, the more motivated the child is to be responsible, which eases some of the parent's worries and negative feelings. As you dedicate yourself to looking at your kid through a clear lens, you will get better at knowing when to step in, and when to leave it be.

This book is heavy in addressing the counterproductive aspects of scolding and over-control and how those negatively impact children. I also assume you do not want to potentially raise incompetent kids or spoiled brats. Therefore, do not do for your children what they can do for themselves. There is a difference between being nice and enabling.

For example, I am not fostering healthy development by carrying my child's backpack, waking up my teenager for school, buying that kid whatever is desired, fixing every meal, allowing profanity at home, doing my adolescent's laundry, issuing minimal to zero chores, being the kid's personal assistant, or fighting every battle. So remember to try and stay respectful with your words, *and,* your overall "empowering not enabling" parental style. When we enable we are making it about the parent, not the child's proper development. Most of you already know how harmful this enabling stuff can be, but sometimes it's good to hear it from someone else.

It is also particularly important to recognize that you must take care of yourself. Parenting is a boundless challenge, and a worn-out version of you is not good. Set date nights. Find good babysitters. Regularly send your children to camps or reputable community centers/programs. Let your kids sleep over at solid relatives' and friends' houses. Establish some comfort in thinking "Everything is going to be okay" as you create breaks to help refuel your mind and body. Do not take this lightly. You also deserve to enjoy life. There's an old saying in the mental health industry that has significant truth to it: *Children are only as healthy as their parents.*

This might help sum up a major theme of this chapter.

<u>Tri-C Mission Statement:</u> It is no longer about me; it is my child's turn. Every moment I'm with my kid, I must take the high road and appropriately meet my child's developmental needs instead of my wants. I must understand and accept my kid as a person, and I must find my child's frequencies to communicate effectively, coaxing this individual to continuously be open to my parenting. I chose to give up a lot when I became a parent. This is my responsibility. I owe it to my kid and to the world to raise a good soul.

In conclusion, your appropriate Tri-C interactions will inspire your child (no matter what age) to return the respect, recognize the profit of honoring you and the relationship, grant you genuine credibility, and develop the tools to meet realistic expectations. For some of you this might sound too good to be true, but when you diligently start the process of Tri-C and stay on course—unless there is some kind of moderate to significant emotional or mental disorder present—things will undoubtedly improve. Keep reading.

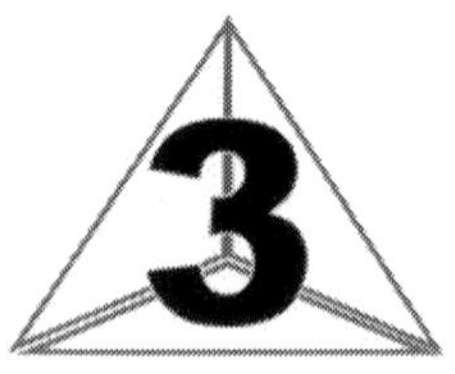

Clear

Before we discuss in detail looking at your child clearly and communicating clear, reasonable expectations, I want to mention something else about Tri-C. Earlier I stated that athletes *must* master the fundamentals to have any chance at serious success, and once that is achieved, they can personally customize their approach to the game.

Again, it's the same for parenting. You and your kid are different from other parent-child pairings, and I can't (nor do I want to) instruct you on how to manage every detail of child-rearing. There are some good parenting books already in publication, but because many of them can be long-winded and saturate the reader with unnecessary statistics, personal stories, graphs, references, techniques, and charts, the parent gets overloaded and justifiably collapses.

Although I will address some of the major issues, and a few standard parenting concepts in this book might appear somewhat familiar, your child will still need you to trust yourself and tap into your natural instincts as to what appropriate parenting is and is not. Tri-C is not a far-reaching, parenting master plan to overwhelm or "fix" you, nor is it an amateur, Whac-A-Mole approach from a clever mom or dad who is trying to tell you what's what, and how you should superficially react to your kid's negative behavior. Tri-C is a formal system: a methodology of parenting specifically designed to soak into your core, provide you a more in-depth clinical, yet simple understanding of your child, and allow you to implement enduring foundational change where necessary.

Of course you'll experience a learning curve and that's totally normal. As long as your youngster knows you are committed to being a rock-solid parent, and you eventually master the economic yet powerful Tri-C fundamentals, your parenting confidence will grow. Tri-C helps you tip the scales, so eventually the vast majority of your communication with your kid is not administrative (because it doesn't have to be), and you and your child get to consistently enjoy each other's company! And that is the entire point!

However, after reading this book, if you think there are certain areas of parenting you're still not quite sure about, you can find plenty of specified blogs, articles, podcasts, etc. by qualified medical and mental health professionals who should be able to help. And no one can make you commit to become a great parent; that dedication has to come from inside you. I also recognize some of you reading this might struggle with obtaining any type of support, or you might have significant challenges based on the area or neighborhood in which you live. So know that Tri-C is merely constructed to best show you how to individually parent, as I've tried to create an approach that compensates for as many external obstacles as possible.

Meeting Expectations

This entire concept is big, so here we go. If the kid is choosing to meet a responsibility, then fortunately the parent does not need to intervene. For example, if your darling child independently wakes up in the morning, has breakfast, and gets ready on time for school, no parenting is required. Your kid realizes there is value in performing that duty. You do not have to needlessly remind (control) that person about anything, as that would generate negative feelings towards you.

However, we know kids are not as mature as adults, and do not always choose to meet reasonable expectations because what they want and what parents want aren't always the same things. In other words, there will be some natural, built-in friction. That's fine—we wouldn't expect otherwise—we just have to get okay with it and deal with it appropriately. Happily for some parents, their responsible children seem to value meeting the majority of normal requirements. There is occasional pushback and mischievousness, but not a lot; they understand it's in their best interest to do what's asked. Other kids, not so much.

So what happens when people don't effectively learn how to meet responsibilities? The real world beats them down. You do not want any of your children to take that kind of beating. Therefore, it is your assignment to help your kid(s) "connect the dots," or in other words, understand more clearly what's being communicated and see the merit in doing what's required.

But first, it's incredibly important to accurately identify what type of young human you've got on your hands. Not only have I engaged in countless conversations in my office with frustrated parents about this, but also the Q & A segment of my seminars often evolve into back-and forth discussions encouraging parents to hone their ability to look at their kid clearly, and stop fantasizing that their child will naturally want to act more mature or agreeable. I also see parents who regrettably want their child to be someone or something that young person is not.

For example, expecting a non-athletic kid to be a starter on the football team, a hard-headed child to have big-picture thinking, or a non-brainiac kid to make National Honor Society isn't fair. Therefore, Tri-C dictates that if you can perceive your child objectively, your expectations of that individual's degree of life skills, level of maturity, and willingness to comply will become accurate. As the parent, you'll dedicate your efforts to shaping the clay you've got and build upon your child's natural strengths (build, build, build), not wish for a different or "better" piece of clay to mold.

Now, what I'm about to state is a very important parenting fundamental. Regardless of how your child is wired, you will create and staunchly maintain normal, reasonable expectations. And of course, the expectations will expand as the child grows older. It's the kid's level of maturity and willingness to meet requirements that gets parents confused and frustrated. The odds of your kid being receptive to your coaching/development and meeting expectations are based on three things: 1) the specific words and delivery used in how you communicate, 2) your remarkable consistency, and 3) the nature of the relationship. Welcome to Tri-C world.

Let's begin with a general example:

Parent: Turn off that video game and come set the table.
Child doesn't respond.
Parent: Hey, let's go. Come on.
Child: In a minute...
Parent: I said right now.
Child remains glued to the screen.
Parent yells: Turn off that stupid game! Why don't you mind me!
Child: Chill out! I'm coming! Sheesh!
Now upset, the parent feels disrespected and takes it personally after years of occasional (and normal) childhood non-compliance.
Parent: I don't understand why you won't just do what I say! I cook you dinner and you don't even care!

This improperly acting parent is failing to consider the audience. Dr. Gary Landreth, one of the masters of child-centered play therapy (a very effective style of therapy for younger children when executed correctly), stated parents must be careful not to view the kid as a "miniature adult," as expectations will rarely be met when that happens. When unrealistic expectations are not met, frustration strikes, compelling parents to "strike out" at their child. Very destructive.

Again, when we choose to become parents it is no longer about us (*you hurt my feelings!*). It's about: *what does my child need from me right now so I can appropriately accomplish the two primary parental tasks: to protect and to develop?* Although this particular scenario doesn't involve "to protect," how could the parent better accept the kid's normal level of maturity, communicate more effectively to uphold the positive relationship, and fulfill the task of promoting healthy development (the kid learning the value of cooperation, responsibility, commitment, and mindfulness)?

> Parent: Would you please turn off your game and come set the table?
> Child doesn't respond.
> Parent: Hey dude, let's go.
> Child: In a minute.
> Parent: Now, please.
> Child is transfixed.
> Parent: Come on, it's ready.
> Child remains unresponsive.
> Parent DOES NOT feel disrespected and states in a low tone of voice: If you choose to not come set the table, you'll choose to not play video games tomorrow.
> *Child jumps up and sets the table.*

This basic example somewhat reflects a classic *Parenting with Love and Logic* dialogue approach. It works smoothly with naturally agreeable kids because they understand the expectation is fair and the parent proposed a reasonable arrangement. The reason it works smoothly with headstrong kids (once they ultimately realize their parent means business) is not only because of the fairness and black-and-whiteness of the requirement (with no room for loopholes or confusion), but also because the parent preserved the connected relationship. The parent showed a clear understanding that the recipient is just a kid who does not have the maturity of an adult, and the parent cared about communicating respectfully so the youngster would be receptive to meet the expectation.

The bottom line: *it worked.* The child performed the task and the parent maintained credibility. The sensible, skilled parent honored an effective strategy instead of honoring the common, inappropriate default of wishing the kid were a certain way. To allow your child to hurt your feelings or wish that young human could magically be more mature is a huge no-no.

Nearly all children know the differences between good/bad, right/wrong, fair/unfair, and reasonable/ unreasonable—do not think otherwise. Although your kids understand your requirements are "normal" and cannot justifiably argue with them, again, they might not like them. Considerate, mindful children can navigate the dynamic of *what I want vs. what the parent wants* fairly easily. Strong-willed kids seem to struggle with this "blending their world and the real world" concept, and they absolutely need the adult to view them through the correct maturity and willingness-to-comply lens.

If a short-sighted child often wrestles with the concept of cooperation, the parent must learn that always going hard at the kid in a traditional "I say jump, you say how high" approach **does not work**. Because the adult clearly has all the power, it boils down to the parent setting a new mental recalibration: change the lens to perceive the child objectively, minimize frustration, and learn to exercise authority in a constructive way.

Like I suggested earlier, some kids might have a disorder like anxiety, ADHD, a negligible degree of autism-like traits (e.g., quirky, rigid thinking, does not adjust easily, and somewhat short on empathy, maturity, social awareness, and mindfulness), or depression (people who are depressed can regularly experience periods of anger or "I don't care," and that is real). These diagnoses can all oppose our ability to function well or demonstrate a willingness to be agreeable.

And regarding ADHD kiddos, an impressive amount of these individuals tend to have a noticeable amount of immaturity, natural impulsiveness, forgetfulness, and stubbornness—all characteristics which hinder awareness and push parents to madness. Parents of an ADHD child must exercise great patience and never dismiss the reality that this mental/learning difference creates challenges. I once heard a tired yet undaunted mom smile and say, "My five-year-old son probably thinks his last name is 'Stop!'"

The short-tempered frustration of a parent directed towards an impulsive and forgetful kid creates more issues, which we're trying to eliminate. Parents of an ADHD child must loyally stay in the business of being understanding, and not be seduced by their own anger and disappointment. Because if they chronically give into their inaccurate expectations, the relationship ends up in the sewer. So long, successful parenting.

Also, a child might have more than one formal diagnosis (which we call comorbidity) that requires extensive understanding and a parent's possible need to find professional help. This is another reason why it's critical you perceive your young human accurately. And, the better you accurately perceive your kid, the more you'll have clear back-and-forth conversations.

Reminder: If Tri-C isn't working after full-blown, proper implementation within a few months, then I encourage you to seek help. Most likely there is something bigger that is causing problems. Ask your child's pediatrician and school counselor what they suggest, whether it's connecting with a good therapist who treats kids, or if there are any programs or treatment centers in your community.

Now, let's talk about parenting predicaments that might be a little more difficult. When our kid is choosing to act defiantly in some way, it is first our responsibility to stay calm (you'll train yourself, unless you already do stay calm), create respectful dialogue, and try to understand why. Asking "why" is important and will be discussed in more detail shortly.

If you stay unfazed and open a potential powder keg interaction using a conversational, concerned question like, "Hey man, what's up?" you've created a specific, non-defensive delivery of two things:

1. I'm being super cool about this and you are not (and nobody likes to be the you-know-what).
2. We are not going to argue, and I'm actually curious—not shaming, sarcastic, or condescending—as to why you're choosing to act this way.

In other words, the stage has been appropriately set for a chat, not a fight. (Know this: if your kid is somewhat rigid-minded, that person most likely cannot effectively process your sarcasm; it is too gray. The individual can probably dish it out but can't take it, so consider eliminating it entirely from your dialogue—it can too easily be misconstrued and hurtful.)

If your earnest questioning works and the innately intractable child has a flash of maturity and complies, that's a nice win-win. But if your kid doesn't have enough internal motivation to meet the expectation and **talk is cheap** (typical with a hard-headed child), and this person needs an actual consequence to reach an important understanding, then you will now create enough external motivation for your kid to realize doing what's asked is a much better option. As words and concepts tend to be abstract and can be conveniently misinterpreted by the child, this approach is very black and white—just like how a stubborn individual tends to see the world.

Also, rewards are great motivators as long as they're used fittingly. Tap into your natural instincts on when to offer a reward to inspire your child to meet an expectation. Do not be reluctant to do this, because with consequences and rewards, we're just shaping behavior.

But, be aware that if you set the appropriate reward too far in the future, some children can't "see it," and it will lose its draw. Towards the end of the day or week is good for most younger kids, and for tweens & teens you can push the prize out a bit further.

However, if a reward for a certain circumstance is not suitable or won't do the trick, you can issue a fair consequence that is more powerful to your child than upholding the defiance. Many parents implement a reward-consequence combo if the situation calls for it, meaning the child's choice of behavior will bring either a gift or a punishment—just like in the real world.

Let's have a little fun. Here's a consequence only example. Your uninspired tween "agrees" to fold and put away clothes every Monday. It's not happening. You justifiably feel irritated. You can:

A) Quarrel, yell, and punish, which is highly undesirable and drives the kid to become even more insufferable.
B) Sincerely (not angrily) ask "why" your child is choosing not to honor your request.

If you choose B, then hopefully your kid will have a self-aware, mature realization of "I don't want to do this, but I know I need to" and the task is performed. However, in the early stages of Tri-C implementation, you might unfortunately get some ill-mannered answer in the spirit of, "Because it's stupid and I don't care about my clothes being folded."

If that's the case, do not argue. *Gas! Fire! Boom! Bad!* Your naturally challenging child knows this requirement is fair but is trying to get away with not doing it for whatever reason. Therefore, by remaining composed and keeping this interaction conversational (this is just a game you're playing—try not to get wound up or take any of this personally as you squirt water on the fire, not spray it with gasoline), you will stay in the reasonable part of your brain. Your kid will think, *Uh-oh*, and feel distressed upon seeing you're not going to be drawn into a debate, and the opportunity to get you upset or to exercise control is vanishing. I once had a teenager in my office smile and admit that if he can get his mom to argue, she's stepped into "his territory."

So, after the laughable, defiant answer to your question, "Why are you choosing not to fold and put away the clothes?" you will ask again. And if refusal is the *stance du jour*, you'll coolly say, "You can choose to do it, or you can choose to lose your electronics the rest of the day and tomorrow."

You both know this is not an end-of-the-world punishment your child might choose to suffer, but now it's officially become a *contest*. Your kid may become angry and attempt to defend the chosen position and say more dumb things like, "Why do you care? They're my clothes!"

To that, you will tonelessly counter, "We've already discussed this, but if you need me to tell you once more, I will." (Your child always has the right to ask why. Regardless of "an attitude" or not, never respond with "Because I said so." That is discounting and disrespectful, and it damages the relationship which you are always upholding, and you're always upholding the relationship because you love your child no matter what and because you are learning that a maintained, positive connection makes parenting five thousand times easier. So instead, address the kid's surly remark.)

Your exasperated youngster will continue to try and argue; however, you will keep this encounter in perspective, not take the kid seriously, and not respond.

Your kid will gawk at you in anticipation of your retort.

You will maintain an expressionless face.

Your child will react to your non-provoked stance with another dopey, disrespectful comeback.

Then, as you casually return to what you were doing and not allow this to break into a death spiral, you'll say, "We don't talk like that to each other in this family. Try again. And let me know what you decide."

If your kid continues to be contentious, you must simply ignore it or respond with a very brief, canned answer. This can be difficult until you learn how, but the lesson is coming soon. Your child will make a brutish attempt to goad you, and every fiber of you will be tempted to jump into the ring, go toe-to-toe, and cut that joker down to size. If you do ignite or argue, you lose, child wins. Remember, **this is comedy hour and not to be taken seriously.**

Therefore, if you stay calm and quiet, you will experience victory! You'll get to witness the beauty of your powerless tween taste bitter defeat as the knucklehead skulks off and is left with a wrenching decision to either fold and put away the clothes, or lose privileges. This is a glorious and potentially defining moment. And, if this is one of your early encounters with this type of parenting strategy, your kid might not perform the task at hand due to inherent willfulness, unwillingness to lose, and hopes that you won't actually administer the consequence.

But you *will* enact the consequence, and your child will get upset again. So what? Unless the kid is going to do something dangerous like jump out the window, go ahead and let that goober throw a fit. You can either sit there and watch the circus act, or walk out. You're creating a new precedent for *all* situations like this. The more you uphold this protocol, the smoother overall parenting eventually becomes. And because you exhibited such composure throughout the entire exchange, your child justifiably can't be mad at you and wrongly shift some of the blame.

Take this approach every time because consistency is the

name of the game—I can't reemphasize this enough. Discouraged parents tell me they've tried a "soft" approach and proclaim it isn't effective. Sometimes I actually have to lure them back to feeling hopeful and reinforce that now that they are learning a new parenting method, they can start to experience success.

But sometimes in initial parent sessions I'll hear, "We've already done all that, and it still doesn't work."

And what I'd like to say back to them is, *Yes it does—you're just not doing it right.* But of course I don't say that. What I will do is teach them to execute the Tri-C system exactly. Understand this, especially when you first begin Tri-C: You must embrace this philosophy, be maddeningly consistent, relentlessly uphold your new, mature mindset, and execute this productive process, just like it is described in these pages. Do not waiver or give up. Your subordinate kid will ultimately come around because that young person will have no choice with your "soft" yet firmly uniform approach. When defiance appears, your Tri-C application and the steady stream of potentially losing privileges or delivered consequences will become so utterly convincing that it will override your child's need to be obstinate sooner than later.

But if you get outwardly frustrated and communicate harshly at any time, you will disrupt the regimen. Maintaining composure is a significant element of Tri-C. Stay as unmoved as you can rather than getting suckered into a heated argument or blowing up, or you will provide your kid more material to build the dreaded spite wedge you are about to discover in the next section. So stay cool, do not get manipulated, and do not take yourself or the kid seriously.

You'll know it's working when your child eventually begins to mirror your responses, "I know. If I choose to not to put away my clothes (or whatever the task happens to be), I choose to blah, blah, blah. I get it." Smiles all around.

The Spite Wedge and Magic Wand

A common occurrence I see in my office is when traditional-minded parents bring in their "I like to do things my way" kid because life at home is getting worse. A child who was a bit temperamental when younger has now become a moderately frustrated and confused adolescent. This budding teenager (or possible tween) who never seemed too deeply rooted in a surplus of empathy is feeling more formidable and trying to flex a growing, somewhat non-compromising agenda. The conventional parents are trying to force a circle into a square peg, which is the worst thing they can do. Parents push. Kid gets mad. Parents push harder. Kid becomes more unmanageable.

The first time a child chooses to be disrespectful or test the waters and blatantly refuses to do what's asked, we parents naturally respond with some degree of firmness, such as, "Let me go ahead and make something perfectly clear: it is not a good idea to defy me, you little devil." But when our "employee" whom we can't fire (and the child knows it) begins to demonstrate a pattern of unmistakable defiance, it becomes somewhat bewildering. We simply can't believe it.

So what happens then? Angered parents take this relationship down the wrong path as tensions continue to mount and life at home becomes difficult. This is the creation of what I call the "spite wedge." Convincing a young human to continuously want to mind is hard enough without bitterness involved.

And how about this one? Why can a kid act good at school but demon-like at home? Because at school, which has structure, consistency, a clear hierarchy, and peer witnesses, the student knows trying to get away with ludicrous behavior is out of the question due to hardened rules and consequences, and, potential ridicule from peers. However, at home, where it's safe and prohibited actions are "tolerated," mild inappropriate behavior can eventually explode into over the top, preposterous behavior—the gloves can come off completely.

Nonetheless, if a somewhat willful child has become unmovable at home and is now regularly wanting to fight, or throw a tantrum, or shut down rather than be agreeable, then the spite wedge acts as a juvenile barrier the kid embraces to keep parents off-balance and prevent them from imposing more expectations. The young, unenlightened human will act passive-aggressive and/or outwardly rebellious, and has yet to realize life is so much more pleasant when parent-imposed requirements are met.

Parents are real-world agents who administer real-world expectations and who regularly keep youngsters from getting their way. Therefore, headstrong kids can falsely blame or punish the adult(s) for their own personal frustrations obtained from both inside and outside the home. They also tend to experience more overall frustrations than the next kid. Home unfortunately becomes a "safe" battleground, and the parents become the convenient target because steadily perturbed kids often feel like they need a scapegoat or punching bag.

In other words, in the child's mind, it's easier to be the misunderstood kid who has "mean" parents. Very immature thinking. In order to fix this, you will essentially disassemble an unproductive home template, and instead rebuild a new, functional model. If "home is a microcosm of society" and you can ultimately create a productive, happy home, the fruits of your labor will most likely result in a positive and responsible-acting kid who consistently likes you, feels more self-confident, and operates more successfully everywhere. Great wins all around.

To begin this entire process, first we start by looking at the vexed kid and the situation clearly and applying specific language to remove the spite wedge. Time for the Tri-C magic wand, where half the spell will be cast on you, the other half on the child.

Remember, no matter what your kid tries to say or do to convince you otherwise (young humans can manipulate, lie, deflect, flip out, and generate amazing excuses and distractions), you understand that regardless of what the expectation might be, your child *knows* it is fair but doesn't want to do it. Do not think otherwise.

Allow me to reemphasize this part, because this challenging concept must be seared into your brain: in many situations, your first step will be to ask *why* the defiant behavior is being chosen, not highlight your anger or the kid's actual behavior. Absorb this self-administered spell when your child is being non-compliant or has broken a rule, as you will be inclined to get upset and make things worse. (Please note: even naturally cooperative kids can sometimes appear argumentative, ask in an unmannerly way why they have to do something, or have a negative attitude—these resistant-looking reactions do not necessarily indicate there's a spite wedge.)

Regardless, the spell cast on you will remind you not to get flustered and **not to take what this kid says or does personally,** and that the pure nature of effective parenting is a process which *must be played out fully*. With people, one thing leads to another leads to another—either a more positive or more negative set of actions will create a particular, everlasting outcome. Regarding the process of productive parenting, the arrangement of measures you execute calls for your adult maturity to activate and carry out the entire situation in an appropriate way (every time), achieving a fundamental Tri-C goal: help the kid connect some valuable dots without damaging parental credibility.

If the parent's resume has a noticeable history of forceful interactions due to prolonged frustration, the kid's spite wedge is most likely in full effect. The parent has made it easy for this child to be oppositional in some capacity. The adult must undo what has been fostered.

Therefore, if your kid is coughing, you don't focus on the act of coughing; you focus on what is causing the cough. For example, if your teen keeps choosing to say inappropriate things in the presence of the younger siblings (i.e., the cough), you will say to yourself:

let the Tri-C process begin.

Instead of getting angry, you will mildly ask "why" this is still happening. Well, you know it's most likely happening because the immature adolescent thinks it's funny, wants to demonstrate some defiance, possibly reinforce the spite wedge, and get a rise out of you due to plausible built-up resentment (i.e., the negative elements which are the root of the cough).

Addressing this type of problem is easy. I declare it's easy because you will refrain from any negative emotion throughout the brief interaction, and execute a concise, distinct prescription: Magic wand—*activate!*

After you casually ask the malcontent "why" it's still going on, and your child has no legitimate answer, you, simply being the unruffled parent will say, "If you keep choosing to say inappropriate things at home (and you've already seen this effective policy delivered in earlier examples—because it works), you'll choose to lose your phone for the day." (Or screen time, or going over to your friends, or whatever reasonable consequence you decide.) The young contestant might try to fortify the spite wedge with an attempted argument—especially if you've had to execute a consequence—but you're done with this game show. And when I say done, I mean *done*. Do not continue the exchange or cave in.

Or let's say the kid snuck out and you busted that desperado. This situation is a little more complex. What do you do? For this particular infraction, you won't waste much dialogue on the hazards of kids roaming the streets after dark. The young culprit already knew it was wrong and dangerous, so it will get maybe a 30-second review. Therefore, the primary bulk of your approach **will not** be, "I can't believe you did that! You're in so much freaking trouble!" (You would be focusing on the "cough.") Your objective is, again, to cast the spell on yourself as you get poised, address the "cause of the cough," and start with, "Why did you choose to do that?" *(Because it's fun and I hoped to get away with it, that's why.)*

This approach works magic in several ways. It eliminates potential friction that leads to arguments, more excuses, lies, or deflections, and the child knows it. *Ah, rats*! the kid thinks when the spell has been cast and a) it is time to accept responsibility for the chosen behavior, b) no spite wedge enhancement will take place tonight, and c) a consequence is coming that is admittedly well-deserved. You're also homing in on who the kid is (i.e., personal character), because by asking "why," you are taking a clear yet non-threatening approach of "This is not acceptable behavior" rather than "You will follow my rules, or else!" In other words, you are effectively addressing the source of the issue. If you unnecessarily and destructively yell then punish, you're increasing the wedge the kid might be wanting to reinforce. Down you go as you sabotage your parenting, blow up the process, and make the child more difficult to deal with now and in the future. Agony.

Here's another one: "Why didn't you do your homework?"

If the oblivious or brooding student means to be honest, you would probably hear, "Because I didn't want to." Instead, the response is nearly always some ridiculous excuse or "I don't know," which then potentially devolves into a squabble. But if you disregard the magic wand, then I'll have to ask you, "Why are you arguing?" Remember:

1. Your kid knows always doing homework is a real-world requirement that demonstrates responsible behavior.
2. You know almost all kids hate homework.
3. Arguments are destructive to relationships. Do not argue—this is a Tri-C fundamental.
4. The parent is in charge, the kid has no power cards, and all parties understand this.
5. You genuinely do want to know the reason and will address the kid's decision-making ability, not hammer the kid nor

emphasize the non-compliant behavior. If there actually is a legitimate reason or misunderstanding, then it becomes a conversation between the parent and child. No hurtful, false allegations are made. Always try to honor "blood is thicker than water." Try not to immediately jump to conclusions—allow the kid the chance to rightfully explain. Be patient during these conversations because the truth will almost always be revealed. And if the truth is because the youngster broke a rule or chose to be irresponsible, then appropriately address that.

If the parent entertains the idea of arguing or instantly starts slinging indictments, then this exchange goes down an entirely different avenue. The focus becomes the child's excuses or "symptoms" instead of the reason. When we argue, we tend to get heated, and when we get heated we say hurtful things which puncture the child's self-worth.

Well, guess what? Those words will injure the relationship which is a direct violation of Tri-C. When the relationship takes on too much damage, the kid starts to disrespect the adult. And when the kid loses respect for the parent, credibility disappears.

Whoops.

If the adult repeatedly gets outwardly upset at the child instead of keeping everything in Tri-C mode, the parent cannot effectively uphold the two primary parental tasks—to protect and to develop—because the youngster either becomes beat-down or doesn't care anymore what comes out of the parent's mouth. The spite wedge becomes bigger than the Great Wall of China.

Therefore, if you choose to stay calm, back your kid into a soft corner, and earnestly ask "why" (without getting angry) nearly every time an abject choice is made:

A) You won't get drawn into an argument.

B) The kid cannot justifiably get mad at you and develop the spite wedge.
C) You productively challenge the unfavorable behavior instead of getting too controlling, bossy, or forceful.
D) The appropriate consequence (or briefly spoken reminder if the infraction wasn't too bad) will do the job.

Allow me to reemphasize the part regarding more noteworthy transgressions: *the punishment will do the talking for you.* If your delivered consequence is painful enough, there is no legitimate reason for you to get angry or lecture and lose credibility. For example, if you choose to speed down the road and a police officer writes you a $300 ticket, the cop doesn't need to lambast you—that would agitate you and make you want to unjustifiably project some of the blame onto the officer and not accept full responsibility. It's just like what our kids do to us when we scold and continuously punish. Can you say "spite wedge?" However, if the cop firsts sincerely asks "why" you're speeding and acts courteous, it becomes especially difficult to not accept ownership of your actions.

I know that we adults are supposed to be better than hurtfully chastising our very own children, but I also know sometimes it's hard not to do that when our kids are provoking the crud out of us. If this is an area of potential cerebral rewiring for you, please be patient with yourself as you integrate Tri-C into your *modus operandi.* Learn to relax, and trust that the rightful delivery of earned consequences will indeed do the trick. Oh, and a $300 ticket? *Ouch.* Back-to-back $300 tickets? *Oh, man.* Three in a row? *Holy cow. You are done speeding.*

Here's a quick example of healthy parenting. This "effectively convincing the child to follow their rules" illustration demonstrates the parents are more interested in maintaining a good relationship than flaunting insensitive dominance.

Young teenager likes to ride his bike with his friends during the summer. They'll cruise around and hit a park or two, play ball, and visit different houses for lunch, video game action, etc. As this kid becomes more inconsistent with informing his folks of his whereabouts, the parents grow frustrated because they already addressed this issue, and have asked the kid to be more communicative. Kid is cavalier about the whole thing, which causes the mom and dad to become even more flustered. These parents can either build the spite wedge and give in to their anger—yell, lecture, and over-punish, or wave the magic wand.

Mom: Hey. Why aren't you letting us know where you are? (Parents stay relaxed as they cast a spell on themselves and first ask "why.")
Kid: Are you talking about yesterday?
Mom: Yes. I didn't hear from you for five hours. You wouldn't respond to my calls and texts, and I've asked you to be better about this.
Kid: We were playing a new video game at Jake's.
Dad: Did you not have your phone with you?
Kid conjures a quick excuse: Uh, I think it was dead, and I was charging it in the other room.
Dad: It was also late. And getting dark outside. You know to be home before sunset, or at least check in and see if we're having dinner as a family. (Dad keeps it at volume "2"—no gasoline.)
Kid smirks: Hmm. I guess I just forgot.
Mom does a nice job not getting too upset with the cheekiness, grins, and inserts a little humor: Well I tell you what, Captain Amnesia. If you choose to not be more responsible and let us know where you are, or choose to not come home on time, you'll choose to be grounded and lose your devices the next day. (Mom gives him the responsibility and sets a concrete, potential consequence.)

Kid receives the other half of the spell (able to stay in the reasonable part of his brain because his parents are not expressing any inflated frustration), remembers who's in charge, drops the arrogance, and understands this is a just rule: Okay. Sorry.

To summarize, the parents remained calm, didn't lecture, didn't go straight to a punishment, and gave their kid the opportunity to demonstrate responsibility. These two paralleled adults created an appropriate condition where their son could choose his outcome. They also understood the importance of maintaining a unified parental front regarding all expectations, rewards, and consequences. If you're not sure you agree on an issue, go ahead and agree with the initial ruling, then discuss behind closed doors if modification is needed.

Also, please do not undermine your partner, inappropriately overshare with the child, try to win favor, or get into fights in the presence of your kiddo. These horribly selfish actions all cause massive problems. *Massive.*

The "lazy" parental response towards this kid would've been to express an exaggerated degree of anger. However, a willful child can get defensive easily if responded to coarsely, and can quickly lose sight of the parents justifiably being upset when they're trying to reinforce reasonable rules. The kid's focus becomes defending oneself instead of accepting responsibility, which then usually metastasizes into an argument, which then enhances the spite wedge.

This is why I keep reiterating the value of parents looking at hardheaded children realistically, and not continually acting "put out" when these kids are doing something wrong. And of course these kiddos are going to somewhat regularly "act wrong" because, again, stubborn individuals are inherently driven to want what they want more than recognize the value in understanding what others want—they can't help it. And this selfish-looking attitude typically doesn't go over well with other humans, which causes negative responses towards these children, which then causes negative feelings about themselves. This is not good, especially if it becomes a lifelong thing.

Therefore, because a child who is lacking in interpersonal skills and flexible thinking can struggle to act appropriately regarding certain social interactions, and grapple to meet certain real-world standards, the parents' duty "to develop" (instead of getting upset) throughout all of upbringing will steadily come into play. Regardless of whether you've got a willful child or not, the last thing you want is for your kid to experience a lifetime of negative responses from people (which absolutely cannot start with you) because your child never learned from you how to interpret information more accurately, navigate life more constructively, and become more mindful of others.

Now, here's a short and sweet example that demonstrates two different parenting applications, and although it highlights a kid who is not skilled in the "cooperation department," these contrasting approaches and their effects (especially if exercised regularly) will significantly impact any child.

A family is out to dinner. The tween daughter is hogging all the queso. The parents understand how she's genetically predisposed, but they also know she "knows better." The adults can respond in one of two ways.

A) "What the heck is wrong with you?! Don't you think other people might want some?! Good grief!" This parental response creates in her feelings of anger, embarrassment, shame, and resentment. Damage all around, and down she goes.

B) "Hey sweetie, pass that around. Other people might want

> some." This response is effective, and helps the kid stay in the reasonable part of her brain where she can work on how to jockey situations like this. No spite wedge, no false deflecting, and no shameful feelings created. The parents effectively checked her behavior, and are essentially "in cahoots" with their child as they continually help her learn how to operate more productively in society. In other words, they know she needs some guidance in creating appropriate habits and getting okay with certain real-world principles, and they understand this will naturally take some time, but she'll get there. The parents' determination lies in empowering her to navigate life successfully, not contribute to her defensiveness or negative thoughts and feelings about herself.

As responsible parents, we will undoubtedly have to issue "disliked but necessary" protocols (e.g., curfew, table manners, grades, screen time, chores) and firmly maintain them with respectful interactions that don't build a spite wedge. So remember, your job is not to exercise your overpowering dominance and force your kid to be compliant—your mission is to keep your eye on the prize of developing your child to become a well-functioning adult with strong self-esteem who has learned from you how to move through life successfully.

The Connected Way relationship and solid positioning of healthy standards prohibits our kids from justifiably getting angry, helps them gain the ability to meet real-world responsibilities, and keeps them from constantly seeking cracks in the parenting wall because there aren't any and never will be again. Therefore, if you choose to not communicate appropriately, nor consistently maintain healthy family codes, then you are welcoming one of the most powerful enemies of good parenting. It's called Intermittent Reward. See below.

Intermittent Reward

As the responsible parent trying to raise a responsible kid, it is way too easy to step into the argument trap. You might be growing weary of my spending so much time on this, but because arguing can be so destructive, even after becoming a Tri-C prescriber who knows to be respectful, avoid squabbles, keep your expectations realistic, and recognize that the consequences will do the talking for you, the need to try and convince the child to see it your way can be overpowering.

Throughout parenting, there's plenty of teaching involved. Therefore, when our kid demonstrates a pronounced lack of agreement, we feel the need to force compliance or educate (lecture) that person on why this reasonable standard is in place. *I must convince you to see either the importance of this, or the error of your ways* is our natural, parental instinct talking. And, if a consequence is issued and there is continued pushback, then not only do we become angry, but we also feel pressured to continually defend the punishment. Unfortunately these exchanges can spin into some nasty outcomes.

What we want is for the child to simply yield or admit the poor behavioral choice. How do we achieve that? By eliminating the intermittent reward dynamic.

Intermittent reward (also known as Intermittent Reinforcement, developed by B.F. Skinner, the founder of Behaviorism) is widely regarded by psychology researchers as the most powerful form of motivation on the planet. That's why gambling can be so addictive. Gamblers hope that despite the losses, at some point they are destined to win, and when that finally happens, the thrill is so exhilarating it energizes another attempt.

Kids can fall victim to this addictive mindset when it comes to dealing with their parents. Their tireless determination can occasionally draw us into a harmful argument where they grind us into a pulp and achieve success. We've all been there. And when we finally cave, we reinforce their desire to keep up that strategy. Most children will push for nearly everything, or try to get away with things until they realize they can't anymore. Why wouldn't they?

The parental goal is to end that immature (yet natural) behavior, which is accomplished by being the casino where the kid does not win. We parents do understand that some things are negotiable, but that exchange *feels different*, especially if it does not pertain to an unmet expectation or delivered consequence. Appropriate negotiations are positive relationship-building strategies; we're not making it about the parent, and we are the one showing flexibility.

We're also *listening*. Hopefully our children feel comfortable enough telling us what they want, need, and how they feel. It's up to us to foster respectful conversations and be super reasonable as to what is fair and healthy.

However, if whatever wrongdoing transpired simply because that youngster chose not to meet a regular entrenched standard or is trying to push for something which clearly will not serve in positive development, the young gambler will lose. Every time. And eventually, when the kid finally realizes there will be no wagering on this because of your unwavering consistency, the negative behavior will extinguish. But before the child realizes that gambling (arguing) at the "parent's casino" is in vain, that maverick must continuously lose over and over.

"Okay Brian, but my child is relentless. My kid will goad me, try to take my phone, start crying, scream, punch holes in the walls, and follow me around as I try to get away. It's like I'm dealing with the Terminator! The kid won't stop!"

I know that sounds extreme, but for some of you it's a reality. Follow the Tri-C steps to eradicate that unrelenting behavior, because when it finally ends for good, it's glorious.

Let's do a few more parent-child disagreement examples so we know you've got this. In each of these cases, both parent and child understand the expectation or consequence is fair and/or what the kid desires will not be granted for whatever appropriate reason. Your cunning little card shark begins the unsavory attempt.

Step 1: Relax.
Step 2: Get locked into the logical (non-emotional) part of your brain as you move to...
Step 3: Stay respectful and sheathe that power sword. Remember, this is a game and you both know who has the power; you are merely going to exercise your indisputable command in a purposeful way.
Step 4: If a rule was broken, casually ask, "Why did you choose to do that?"(Cast the spell.)
Step 5: Although your child recognizes the direction you're taking the conversation and still tries to argue (or guilt you, which you will not buy into because you know it's nothing more than juvenile manipulation), you respond with something like, "I know you're bummed, but we've talked about this."

Now, depending on the emotional severity of the kid's behavior, there are two different outcomes. The first few examples represent mild emotional intensity where the kid capitulates without too much uproar. Later, we'll do an example that demonstrates a more difficult affair. You also recognize that "talk is cheap," so there will be no attempt from you to try to convince or lecture—you would be wasting your breath and losing credibility.

Example 1:
Kid: Yes, but Taylor had to take everyone else home, and I didn't want to be a jerk and say I had to go home first, and—
You: You know when your curfew is, you're an hour late and didn't even call or text me. You know the rules. You're grounded for the weekend.

Example 2:
Kid: Everyone else already has a phone, and I'm the only one who doesn't, and—
You: We've already talked about this. You get your phone this summer.
Kid: Yes, but...

Example 3:
Kid: Can't we please swim for five more minutes? Please? I don't see what the big deal is.
You: It's time to get out. Sorry.

From this point forward, you can choose to give no response (not another word, no matter what the child says or does) and resume what you were busy doing, or just sit there and stare at the youngster in solidified silence. You stay unprovoked because we're talking about *a kid*, and you will train yourself to not provide *a kid* any emotional power over you. You get fired up? See ya later.

You also can reply with a very brief ender—something like the signature line from Kuill of *The Mandalorian*, where you'll flatly remark, "I have spoken." Or maybe from Pharaoh Rameses in *The Ten Commandments*, "So it shall be written, so it shall be done." You can choose to respond only once then zip your lip, or repeat the words every time your kid keeps asking or grinding.

I know these lines are sort of hokey, but they work. It's obnoxiously irksome to the young human as you keep restating the emotionless phrase(s). The kid doesn't like it and wants you to **stop**. (Just repeating "I'm sorry" doesn't work. It's too palatable and comes across a bit too gracious.) But the only way to get you to stop saying these excruciatingly irritating responses is for your child to quit asking or quit trying to argue. That's what we call "extinguishing the behavior."

It might take five to fifteen consecutive, separate situations of employing this satisfying tactic, but it will eventually sink in. Your ruffled kid will not be able to hear those words any longer and will come to understand you're not going to crumble. It's the same as going to the casino and playing slots on your favorite machine, but now you lose money on every pull. *Over and over and over.* At some point, reality sets in, you can't take it any longer, and you quit. Maybe down the road you'll cross your fingers and give it a scarce try, but guess what? You'll lose. Again.

But be careful not to use this response strategy haughtily. If you go straight to it, then you will be acting disrespectfully. What I mean is, try not to state these lines as soon as your kid simply asks for something for the first time or when it's your child's first chance to explain behavior. Wait just a little to see if your child keeps trying to argue and isn't willing to accept your healthy parenting decision.

Also, be patient as you learn how to remember to utilize this method. Don't worry, you will recognize when you're being baited, then something in your head will click—*Aha*!—and you will realize, *this is the part where I stop responding and stare at my kid like an android, or repeat "I have spoken."*

Wow! It works!

Here's another emotionally mild example, but this time you have successfully extinguished intermittent reward:

> No electronics in bedrooms on school nights after 9:30 PM. You catch your fourteen-year-old past bedtime with her phone at 11:30 PM. You stand in the doorway and calmly say, "Why are you up, and why do you have your phone?" (Teens need *minimum* eight hours of sleep, more like nine or more; do not compromise on this.) Her excuses and harmless pleading hit you at a dizzying pace. However, you keep your cool and wait for her to stop, which she quickly will, because the magic wand has

been cast on her. She begrudgingly remembers: you've previously issued a warning, you won't be drawn into a feud, and you won't allow her to turn this into something else.

You: Well, dang, you chose to lose your phone for tomorrow. Hand it over.

She sadly relinquishes her treasured device and thinks about how painful it will be the next day without it, but recognizes how respectful you're being. Again, let the consequence do the talking, not you. And of course she will occasionally break rules—she's a kid.

(Always use your leverage as a parent when you need to, whether it's screen privileges, phone, car, or friends. Also remember not to shame, patronize, criticize, condescend, say "I'm disappointed in you," or constantly be sarcastic—those negative communication techniques rip away at a connected relationship. You are your child's hero, and heroes do not hurt their #1 fan.)

Unfortunately, with strong-willed kids, sometimes their emotions can quickly escalate. Why? Three reasons. One, they're not getting what they want, and during this early phase of life, they still struggle with tempering that rigid-minded characteristic, which you are in the business of tackling with Tri-C. Although their intense feelings are real, the sooner in childhood you address this emotional and behavioral overreaction, the faster it is resolved.

(If your kid is already an adolescent, it is still fixable; it will just take longer because the confrontational conduct has become more embedded and normalized. Also, Tri-C effectiveness depends on the level of the child's deep-seeded emotional control—a bipolar or autistic youngster can struggle more to regulate emotions.)

The second reason stubborn kids can emotionally skyrocket is because acting out seems somewhat acceptable as much of their focus is narrowly placed on the self. They can have difficulties recognizing how they impact others and the social importance of how they want others to perceive them. *But wait a minute, Brian.* Earlier you discussed how certain kids can act totally appropriate at school, but completely ridiculous at home. How is that dichotomy possible?

Allow me to restate, and for those of you who have kids like this, this concept is very important to understand. Because deep down they do "know" how to act, but at home feel like they can choose not to act properly because they don't "have" to. As mentioned earlier, lots of these intractable kids not only take out their frustrations at home, remember they also lack somewhat in empathy, which is, to revisit, the inability to adequately A) recognize how they affect the feelings of others (i.e., their parents, who they know will love them no matter what), and B) place value on others' wants. Empathy is a valuable interpersonal trait that works as a governor to help suppress our self-centeredness. It also serves as a social supercharger that significantly helps bolster considerateness towards others. (Empathy is different than sympathy. Sympathy is feeling sorry for someone, and feeling sorry for someone does not keep us from getting what we want.)

Third, they want control (which they feel like they can occasionally fight for at home, or in certain environments, or with certain people), and they want to be right. Inflexible kids unfortunately have the tendency to quickly become irrational and feel threatened, and to try to prove the other person does not have unbridled authority (which of course the parent does, and everyone knows it). Tri-C administered consistently and correctly helps productively address these three issues.

Now, let's proceed to a severe, emotionally intense example involving "your" 16-year-old son:

Kid: I'm not cleaning my bathroom. I'm tired.

You (as you stay resolved, cast the spell, and chuckle under your breath): What's all this, then?

Kid: I'm going to my girlfriend's.

You: You told me you were going to clean the bathroom before the weekend, and it's already Friday night. (You're setting the stage—Act I.)

Kid sees where this is going and dials it up: Leave me alone. I'm sick of you.

(Okay. Your natural instincts probably just shrieked at you to lose your mind on this currently disrespectful-acting kid. The reason your child is behaving like this is because he has some emotional/behavioral challenges, plain and simple, do not forget that. A naturally cooperative, open-minded youngster hardly ever exhibits profound disrespect or sheer insolence. If you flip-out on your strong-willed child? That's right: you lose. Some of your credibility will disintegrate, and as you recall, when you lose credibility, you cannot constructively enact the two primary parental tasks. So here you are, getting into your new Tri-C routine, keeping it together with the realization that you need to exercise your maturity and patience with this child and play out this process fully, knowing ultimately you will win.)

Game time!

You, emotionally unprovoked: Dude. Not a good decision right there.

Kid: I can say whatever I want!

You: We don't yell and scream in this family. What's going on?

Kid: Why do you care?! (He is upset and clearly wants to fight because he feels like he can get away with it, at home, with you. But make no mistake, he is beginning to learn that your Tri-C approach is "The Way.")

You know how to proceed and calmly respond: I care because I'm your parent.

(All you've done up to this point is set an awesome example. You've acted respectfully and tried to get him to holster those pistols.)
Kid: I'm not going to clean the bathroom!
(Child has now made it clear this is simply a case of him choosing to embrace his immature anger and dig in his heels.)
You: I'm sorry, son. So listen. You can choose to do it, or choose to lose your devices for the weekend. (Wham-O. Act II.)
Kid: You can't take my X-Box! I bought it!
You: I can and I will. So what's it going to be?
Kid*:* I hate you! You suck!

At this point, the child either storms off, blows up, or says or does something else inappropriate. You stay logical and do not respond—you've already made your ruling and won. Trying to reason with someone who is feeling exceedingly defensive is almost as ludicrous as trying to reason with a drunk. *Ya know what? Think I'll just circle back when you're sober*. Child realizes you are not going to react to the absurdity and finally (hopefully) calls it a day. If it takes a half-hour of enduring this stand-up act then go microwave yourself some popcorn. Again, you "have spoken."

Do not give in, do not retaliate. Remember, this is an exercise you are engaged in and you are following a course of action to create an eternal, desired outcome. After your kid cools down (because he will eventually move back to the reasonable part of the brain), you can conversationally discuss the unsuitable behavior and what he can do to help control that. You will not allow unbound, unreasonable thinking and wild, inappropriate behavior to normalize. Ever.

Regardless if you have a productive conversation either that day or the next, all screens are still gonzo (Act III). Tomorrow arrives, and your child is wondering if you still mean what you said. You do not mention the infraction or loss of privileges until that subject is broached *by the kid.* Trying to drive home the point or continuing to express your anger, as much as you might want or think you need to, infuriates that person and vandalizes the relationship. Let it sit; your consequence will perform the assignment. Remember, the less you talk, the less chance there is of exacerbating any issues. There is no reason to "add to" or argue. Stay unprovoked, and remember your kid already knows what the deal is and who is in charge—do not feel like you have to keep repeating yourself.

You also understand how this young individual operates; therefore, you know whether this artful dodger will try to sneak a device. Well, guess what? There aren't any devices available to access. You've taken all of them. (This includes taking power cords or turning off the Wi-Fi if necessary. I know that sounds unpleasant for all, but you will do what must be done to set a precedent.) He will either let it lie and understand what has happened, or ask you, "What the heck?"

To that you will respond, "Because you chose not to clean the bathroom and were so disrespectful, like we discussed, you chose to lose all your technology for the weekend." (Don't ground or take privileges away for more than two weeks *regarding nearly any situation.* Two weeks is forever to a kid, and once you get past that marker, the punishment simply becomes monotonous and you've lost what you are trying to accomplish. Also, be specific regarding the conditions of the punishment and the expiration date—eliminate all ambiguity. In other words, don't autocratically say something like, "You'll get your phone back whenever I decide.")

Child might mildly pop off and creep back to his room, or, raise another stink. If the kid freaks again, stay calm, remind yourself to stay pledged to the process, and see how far it goes. This might require much effort on your part, but typically the reaction in this phase is not so radical. He is beginning to realize that throwing tantrums is ineffective and that you are a dealer who never loses, nor does he want another consequence issued.

Hooray! The removal of intermittent reinforcement is under way! Keep in mind, the permanent extinction of this type of reward totally depends on you being consistent, undisturbed, no arguing or lecturing, and a delivered consequence when a rule has been broken. I'm going to state those again. Do not yell. Do not quarrel. Administer an appropriate punishment. Consistency is the part of this process that parents seem to struggle with the most, but all parts must be fully enacted. Without consistency, there is no effective removal of *anything*. Inconsistency fuels intermittent reward *(boo)*. Consistency crushes it.

The steady application of Tri-C sends a very strong message: *Inmates do not run the asylum. I will not be threatened or bullied. I will not acknowledge your ridiculous behavior, and I will administer a consequence (every time) that is much more substantial than your choice to act rebellious or not meet our normal expectations*. Based on your child's degree of immaturity and willfulness, it may take up to six months (six months?! Yes, half a year) before the child chooses to regularly control emotions at home and recognizes that brazenly acting out is no longer worth it. Stay on course, loving and determined parents.

With that being said, unacceptable behavior and kids assuming any control will never be permitted. Ever. Home is not a chaotic madhouse, and the parent-child hierarchy cannot be allowed to shift the other way. You can never compromise on this. Kids do not know what they are doing, and if your children somehow feel you are "equals," or are left to their own devices, catastrophe follows. If you give them an inch they will likely take a mile, and you'll find yourself having to work uphill.

Plus, if "everything starts at home," you are teaching your kids appropriate self-expression and the understanding that screaming, bullying, and losing control will never get them what's wanted in life. At the first sight of any of your children confrontationally pushing a boundary, put a proper Tri-C stop to it. If you are not able to ultimately put a stop to it, then seek some type of outside help, whether it's a qualified mental health professional, or some kind of child advocacy program in your area. And, like we discussed earlier, if some depression and/or substantial anxiety has moved into your child's life, those diagnoses can cause considerable, unjustified anger and frustration.

Effective Timeout: For parents of little kids, the "termination of intermittent reward" is also highly effective. Three-to-six-year-olds can throw amazing fits when they want attention or don't get their way. How do we extinguish that? Step one is to remember that you are being reasonable when you say "no," and your children absolutely know you're being fair. Step two dictates you instantly remind yourself not to get angry, because lots of little tikes flip out or *push-pushpush* until they learn that does not work.

Here's an example: You all are outside playing, but now it's time to come in for lunch. Your kid doesn't want to and starts to resist. You ask or tell again. The tantrum starts, which means the child is moving from the reasonable part of the brain to the limbic part, where it becomes very difficult to think reasonably.

First, you make a swift attempt to stop this cognitive shift by getting down on one knee and stating, "I know you want to stay outside and play with your friends, but it's time for lunch." (Respectfulness!) The kid either moves back into the frontal lobe of logical reasoning and agrees (which, again, happily becomes the standard once Tri-C is *The Standard*) or doesn't and is now deteriorating into full-blown, irrational overload. The child literally cannot think clearly at this point, so don't try to reason, force, beg, or argue with this little person, because that ineffective approach **does not work**.

Since you're a mature adult who recognizes what's happening

and knows how to quickly proceed, you say to your child, "You can choose to come eat, or choose to go to timeout." (However, sometimes the meltdown does not necessarily call for a consequence if it's not a broken rule, defiance issue, or a non-urgent situation—it's a matter of you ignoring the fit and walking away, as in "I will not indulge you, sorry kid!" And for those types of affairs, walk away every time or it WILL NOT STOP.)

Let's say your little stinker continues the blowout and refuses to come in for lunch after you ask once more. Then you'll calmly respond, "I guess you're choosing to go to timeout." Point to a corner and see if the kid goes, but if not, you can still pick up a small child (which you will) and carry that turkey to the designated area. You do not say a word or act angry. Park that kid in the corner and walk away, or sit directly across if you think the child won't stay.

Showdown!

What's going through the kid's mind is one thing, and one ludicrous thing only: *This stinks! It didn't work! I want my way! Arggh!* But the child is also beginning to learn (key word: beginning) that throwing a fit will not achieve what is desired, that you are the reasonable authority figure who will be in charge for eighteen years, and that you will always expect and enforce appropriate behavior. After a minute or two, ask, "Are you ready to eat?" If the squirt says *No!* you will say, "Then we'll just sit here until you're ready." And you will, staying silent, looking around, and being chill.

After another minute or two passes, ask again. What's now going through that little brain is *This is not what I hoped for, and I'm not getting the reaction I expected, but I won't give in!* As the adult, you clearly comprehend this strategy and know you are way more interested in doing what's necessary to end this type of conduct (for good) than losing your patience, so you stay on point and say non-condescendingly, "Let me know when you're ready, because I can sit here all day."

Kid is reluctantly starting to understand you forever mean business as you maintain your steadfast position, do not argue, and do not whip out the flamethrower. You are silent. You execute this process fully because you can outlast your child regarding any predicament. Thankfully, the child will eventually shift back to the reasonable part of the brain and capitulate—which leads us to more talk about consistency.

Consistency: I must revisit this with you, because when your child demonstrates any degree of unmet expectation, you must exercise a parental approach of which consistency is an irreplaceable, top-tier principle. Because if you don't, and instead you happen to cave or scream or spank or argue, then not only will you have to start all over—uggh, as inconsistency is the lifeblood of the dreaded intermittent reward—but also detrimental parental reactions will violate the invaluable Connected Way relationship approach, which you are now committed to upholding.

When various negative childhood behaviors emerge, Tri-C productively addresses and dethrones them. You might need to deliver a Tri-C strategy a solid five times in a row (it might take three, it might take twenty, but we already know this) to extinguish your child's irrational thoughts and negative actions. Your kid will learn that any type of oppositional conduct demonstrated will draw a sound response from you. The most trusted sidekick of Tri-C is consistency. I cannot overstate this enough.

One of the hardest parts of administering a series of effective actions is casting the Tri-C spell on yourself (stay calm, ask "why," and address the root instead of the symptoms) when the resistance begins. So when your kiddo revs it up, activate the magic wand, and get to work.

As the loving parent, you will appropriately do what you must to foster positive behavior and steer your child in the right direction. Again, if Tri-C does not work and your kid continuously refuses to be parented, then do whatever is in your power to seek the correct level of help.

I cannot stress how imperative it is for you to painstakingly uphold healthy family protocols. Earlier I mentioned that children find cracks in the wall. If you currently have some fractures, it's because your fervent kid(s) did a number on you and out-muscled you in the control department. Kids not only develop the spite wedge, but also create land mines where parents become fearful to even ask them to fulfill certain expectations. These scared, conditioned parents tiptoe around, hoping not to upset their overly defensive youngster(s). Never parent out of fear. If you are parenting out of fear, you are being manipulated and have lost control. You must always be in control.

However, as you unwaveringly administer the "end of intermittent reward" program and your respectful delivery of "Expectations will be met, I assure you" policy takes effect, the power will either remain with or shift to its rightful owner: you. I know this sounds controlling, but Tri-C is about appropriate control. You must have your kids' backs until they are old enough to have their own. And here's a great thing: once it has become abundantly clear that you run the show Tri-C style, you can begin to communicate in a more traditional way.

But watch your tone. Hard-headed kids tend to be sensitive as they struggle to accurately interpret all the layers of what is being communicated. If you do find yourself periodically using commanding verbiage (or sarcasm—remember, that is a *Big No*) because you tend to fall into the Compassionate Boss category, try to remember to interact respectfully and to not sound bristly; you are continuously convincing your children to remain a mom or dad fan and to not get defensive too easily.

And now, because you have devoutly implemented Tri-C for a number of months, your child feels remarkably positive towards you (whoopee!) and understands that life is better when conditions are met. (Also, you don't have to die on every hill—just 98 percent of them.) The child actually feels safe to *like* the parent. Deep down, a kid appreciates a caregiver who is responsible and maintains healthy guardrails. It indicates the adult *cares*, which is fortifying and leads your young human to want to communicate more favorably, and consider what is important to the parent instead of rigidly observing only personal wants.

"Hey, time for lunch."

"Okay."

"Can you come fold these clothes?"

"No problem."

And the child's intermittent reward career?

Terminated.

The Rhetorical Question and Follow-Up

If you haven't already, apply these parenting strategies into your regular dialogue with your child. This is as important to remember as the multiplication tables in math. First, the rhetorical question: "Would you do me a favor and put away your shoes?" "What are your thoughts on helping me in the garage this Saturday?" "Would you mind keeping it down while I'm on the phone?" People appreciate being asked instead of being told. Very much. Especially rigid-minded individuals who can misinterpret tone and actual meanings.

It's also nice to include a window of time. "Before you go out with your friends, can you straighten your room?" or "After you're done with your video game, would you feed the dog?"

Parents sometimes tell me they try the polite and timeframe approaches and they don't work. They're not successful because they won't consistently enact the follow-up. *All follow-ups must happen*. As we dig a little further into these conversations, parents then admit this is where they mostly fail. They struggle in the consistency department because executing the follow-up creates more conflict (only at the beginning, until the kid knows the regulation will always be enforced), and/or because it's inconvenient. For instance, now the parents have to micromanage screen time or bedtime, or have a grumpy lout sulking around the house making everyone else miserable, or have to drive their teenager to high school, or maybe the impatient or frustrated parents "just don't want to mess with it." *Hello, intermittent reward.*

If I ask my kid to put away her backpack after she is done watching TV ("Hey, will you put your backpack in your room after your show?"), I know that won't necessarily be priority #1 to that individual. So I'll keep my ears perked because I'm not exactly sure the task will be carried out. Once the program is over, I'll go to her and say, "Looks like that episode is done. Your backpack is waiting."

She says, "Hold on. I was going to watch one more. Can I do it after this?"

As the parent, you can either look at the kid through the incorrect lens and get upset because you wrongly think this child should possess the priorities of a twenty-year-old and "want to" perform this charge, or you stay reserved and tell her the time is now to fulfill the duty (or, let her watch one more then carry out the task). Regardless, if your kid seriously balks, you'll plainly state (you'll recognize this line, and so will she): "If you choose to not put up your backpack, you'll choose to pay me five dollars." That's the follow-up. The super follow-up is when you make her pay because she actually left the scene and didn't do it. (Get the word "choose" deeply implanted into your vernacular.)

To add to the police officer/traffic stop analogy, if you speed down the road and get pulled over and only receive warnings instead of tickets, why would you stop speeding? Especially if you just happen to like to drive fast and you've got a shiny red Porsche that goes 200 MPH. You finally stop speeding when you get an expensive ticket *every time*, or worse yet, lose your license for a while. Now that's painful. And you might not like to admit it, but you totally deserved it.

The rhetorical question (and when fitting, inclusion of a timeframe) helps the youngster feel respected, and feel like there is some personal control over when the duty is executed. Again (and I'm not saying you personally do this), successful child-rearing does not include "just letting things go," or exercising your overwhelming dominance.

And sometimes we see certain parents act bossy towards their own kid when they're around other adults. *Look how much my child respects (fears) me, and see how high-powered I am. (Or stop embarrassing me.)* "Sit up straight." or "Go change clothes!" or "Nope, because I said so." In these situations, the misguided parents have placed more emphasis on their own wants or anxieties instead of their kid's development.

Development? Yes, indeed. Because you're the parent, you are always modeling behavior for your child. Always. Your child sees and hears everything you do and is taking notes, from how you act around your friends, to how you manage your time, to how you treat the dog. If you constantly act high and mighty, you're demonstrating disrespectful communication skills. That's not healthy development. And if you spank your kid, you create two dreadful acts of harmful disservice.

Corporal Punishment: I won't spend a lot of time on this, but what I'm about to state is extremely important to know as I open this can of worms. In 1998, the American Academy of Pediatrics (AAP) formally announced a recommendation: to discourage parents from regularly spanking children as a method of punishment. In 2018, the AAP updated its policy, advising parents to not spank their children at all.

First, hitting generates huge damage to the relationship. *Huge*. We do not like or trust people who strike us—not sure how else I can put that. If you spank, you will never be able to get Tri-C fully incorporated. Second, it creates an endorsement of violence. I do recognize some kids can become so belligerent that a parent feels hitting is the only way to: bring that individual back down to earth, get the kid's attention, or send an overpowering message that declares "I am in charge, and that behavior is not permitted."

I know this is a polarizing subject. Some of you may have an incredibly difficult youngster, and some of you were parented this way. However, that does not make it right or necessary. I'm an old-school guy, but actually delivering a blow to your child because you are so upset or you're trying to make a statement? Or execute a punishment? That's rough, man. Let Tri-C help you feel like you don't have to do that anymore.

As exhibited earlier, for younger kids "timeout" actually does work remarkably well but must be carried out exactly as described until the inappropriate reactions extinguish. And, if you have credibility with your child and the situation (e.g., running into the street) calls for it, you can get eye-to-eye with that little one and give a powerful 20-second stern talk that will undeniably get your small human's attention.

So allow me to encourage you to remember the fundamental concept of continually motivating your children to like you and relate to you. Doing so includes healthy follow-ups, but cannot include spanking. I want you to fully enjoy parenthood and for your kids to massively benefit from how well you've victoriously fostered their positive development. Your children must trust and enjoy you, or your powerful influence will amount to *nothing*.

Partnering

People love to feel included in decision-making conversations, especially if it somehow personally involves them. It provides some ownership, which motivates them to want to fulfill the objective. For children to feel like their parents are respectful enough to "partner" to solve certain issues, explore options, or create some structure at home (black-and-white thinking kids seem to do better with structure and routine—it helps them keep their responsibilities in perspective; in other words, consistently meet family and real-world protocols) is an incredibly effective tool to teach self-responsibility and encourage compliance. Another win-win.

Let's discuss ways to partner with your kid. The rhetorical question and window of time strategies have some partnership qualities, but those don't apply to all situations. Let's put school grades into play as this is a widespread issue. In this example, a theme is developing where your kid, in some fashion, is not doing an adequate job with academic performance. You feel your frustration wanting to emerge.

What are your parental options here? To scold, force, and punish? Sure, you can take that approach, but what does that get you? Nothing productive. Or you can consider looking at your child through a clear lens and realistically determine what the hurdle is. Why is your kid not doing better in school? (Let me reiterate this: ADHD is real, and it's a mighty nemesis of scholastic achievement. If your kid is easily distracted, fights doing homework and/or consistently misses assignments, is disorganized and impulsive, and struggles to focus on things that are not particularly enjoyable, please have this evaluated by a mental health professional or your pediatrician.)

As we now know, step one is to understand the actual reason for the issue. Then, we fittingly influence the kid to connect the dots, and in this example, help the child realize (remember) that making good grades is mega-important. Therefore, in true Tri-C form, first politely inquire "why" and see if there is a valid reason for the poor grades.

If this situation boils down to simple immaturity (not a learning disability or overly difficult material), and if there is a window of time to play with (school is continuous, so there are many windows of opportunity), then you can partner with the child to create a workable solution. This kid—who never seemed to possess much of a sense of urgency—isn't "getting it." And if you try to apply authoritarian force, then you will create more problems. I don't think you are much interested in intensifying problems.

You: What's going on with your schoolwork?
Kid: What are you talking about?
(Got jokes? Awesome.)
You: I looked online and saw some failing grades and missing assignments.
Kid quickly becomes snippy: I told you my teacher hasn't recorded them yet.
You respond with some suitable firmness: Hold the phone there, sporty. I'm not mad, just curious as to what's happening because I see a pattern here.
(You get provoked? That would blow up in your face, game over. Therefore, you are going to try and disarm your child by approaching this as a discussion, not as a thumping. Plus, you've heard the lame "It's the teacher's fault" excuse before. Also, try to never talk for more than 20 seconds at a time. This is an extremely important parenting strategy to commit to. If you go longer you start lecturing, become disrespectful, and lose the child's attention and willingness, which clearly is not good. You can say everything you need to say in 20-second spurts, which helps the kid see it more like a conversation. I'll talk, you'll talk, I'll talk, you'll talk.)
Kid: Well, uh... (Excuse, fib, excuse, fib.)
You: Here's the thing. I don't care when you do your schoolwork, as long as your grades are good and everything is turned in on time. How can this be fixed?" (You are putting the responsibility on the child.)
Kid: Uh, I don't know.
You: Do you need me to help you in some way? Go through

your assignments with you? Check your work? (Kids hate that.)
Kid: No!
You: Whoa there. Are you feeling okay? Anything bad going on?
Kid: No, sorry. I just need to do it...
Parent: Okay, well, should you study and do homework as soon as you get home from school? Or right before or after dinner?
Kid: After dinner.
You: That's fine, but sometimes we eat late because you have practice.
Kid: I guess on practice days, I can do it earlier?

(What's happening is the child is coming to understand that living mostly in the fantasy world of "I'd rather blow off school" is not going to fly. An apathetic approach to academics is unacceptable. Because you're the adult, you will be the one who will adjust and find the "correct broadband" to effectively communicate, prompting the kid to be more receptive.)

You: I'll leave it up to you, but you spend a lot of time on electronics, so here's what I'm thinking. On week days, you know you have only two hours of after-school recreational screen time (and that includes time looking at the phone, not just talking, although hardly anyone under eighteen-years-old seems to talk on the phone, unless it's FaceTime), so I need to do a better job enforcing that. We'll sit down together on Friday afternoons and go online and look at your grades. If everything is turned in and passing, then you'll get to have electronics for the weekend. But if there are missing or failing grades, no devices again until Monday, and that includes your phone. (Concrete communication—no ambiguity, no room for loopholes, and what was said took less than 20 seconds.)
Kid: But it's going to take me more than a week to get my grades

up and everything turned in and for my teacher to record it!
You: I'm not talking about this week, honey; I'm talking about next week.

(As the parent, you have partnered by allowing your kid to choose when to do schoolwork. You have also upheld respectful dialogue and clear expectations. It is now up to the student to choose to fix the grades. If your child effectively addresses the problem, that's great. But if not, well, let's see what happens next.)

Two weeks later...
You: It's been two weeks and there are still zeros posted. (Immaturity reigns.)
Kid: I'm trying!
You: Well, something still isn't working. I don't see you spending much time doing homework.
Kid: Ugh. I'm just sick of school. And my teacher is a moron!
You: Because you chose to disregard school, there's going to be a consequence.
Kid: But that isn't fair!
You: So it shall be written, so it shall be done.
Kid, becoming more irate: Can't I have another week? I mean—
You: I have spoken.
Kid: Oh my gosh! I hate it when you say that!
You (not getting on the emotional elevator with the kid and going up to the 80th floor): Okay then, how about this? You've chosen to lose your electronics this weekend, but next week, with all grades passing and turned in, we'll go out to dinner Friday after we check (reward: good). And remember, for your core classes, I'll pay you for A's at the end of the nine weeks because the world pays for A's (more reward: good). But if it still looks bad, you'll lose your screens again. And if you have to do your

homework online, you'll set up the living room so I can see what you're doing.

The objective for this kid is to learn to be responsible with academics, and we do this by implementing a parenting strategy which creates the best chance for success—in this situation, partnering to give this individual some decision-making ability regarding when to do homework and demonstrate accountability. However, if you are being ultra-understanding and religiously consistent, and this approach still isn't working after a month (and it's not a learning disability), then you might need to see if there's something else interfering—possibly the onset of adolescent depression or maybe some bullying. And I am not so presumptuous as to tell you what your kid's grades need to be, but with that being said, most parents are more satisfied with a hard-earned C than an easy A.

Let's do a few more partnership examples. Here's a brief discussion between a super cool parent and her nine-year-old son:

Parent: You need a haircut.
Kid: It's my hair, I don't want to cut it.
Parent, smiling: You look like a shaggy bum.
Kid: I don't care. I'm not getting it cut.
(The parent knows how the kid is hardwired so no surprise regarding the stubbornness, and both parties know a haircut is imminent.)
Parent: I have an idea. Let's look online and see if there are some styles you might like.
Kid: Okay, I can do that.

Again, as a parent, you do not have to argue and instantly "force" your child to comply; just get attuned to what works.

Here's an example involving an eleven-year-old daughter and her mother in my office. Mom rocked it:

Kid: I don't want to play tennis anymore.
Parent, who already knew interest was strongly fading: What's happening?
Kid: I'm just tired of it. It's not fun.
Parent: Why isn't it fun?
Kid: I don't know. I've been playing since I was six. Just sick of it, I guess.
Parent: Okay. Then what do you want to do?
Kid: What do you mean?
Parent: I think we talked about you committing to the entire season.
Kid: I know. I thought I would still like it, but I don't...
Parent: Hmm. That stinks.
Kid: I'm just done.
Parent: Are you sure?
Kid: Super done.
Parent: You've got like, five weeks left? Can you make it?
Kid groaned: I guess so. (The tween realized her mom meant what she'd said earlier about not quitting before the season ended.)
Parent: If you're not going to play tennis anymore, what do you want to do instead? (Parent was responsibly "developing" her daughter by requiring fulfillment of the commitment, then partnering with her to see if they could agree on a different activity.)
Kid: I can become a professional YouTuber.
Parent: Hmm. What else ya got?
Kid: I knew you were going to say that. (The more predictable a parent, the better.) You mean like a sport or something, don't you?
Parent: That's exactly what I mean. Something physical.

After a few minutes, they agreed on a return to dance—it was something she'd briefly done back in third grade and now some of her good friends were doing it. However, if she discovered it genuinely was not her thing once she had given it an honest chance, she would have to find something else.

I had an old-fashioned dad in my office and his relatively hard-headed, elementary school aged kiddo whom I was treating. As much as he loved his son, he was having a horrible time with this kid's natural non-compliance. He told me he couldn't get his head around the concept of his child not wanting to obey. *(Obey? Were we talking about a dog?)* This youngster would occasionally refuse to meet a regular expectation because he didn't want to, which led to lectures, frustration, anger, arguments, etc. I helped the dad to understand it is *his job* to get his kid to be receptive to his parenting by waving the magic wand, then partnering. After we went through a few examples they could (and eventually did) implement at home (e.g., "What days would you like to put up the dishes?" "Do you want to feed the cat on weekends or weekdays?"), the dad finally came around. Why? Because his child did!

Here's another example. Mom is trying to determine on which summer days next week her older kid must stay home to babysit the younger sibling. This parent could simply tell the big brother which days he has to babysit, but she wants to show respect:

> Parent: I need you to stay home with your sister some next week.
> Kid: Oh man. Really?
> Parent: Your grandmother is going out of town.
> Kid: I thought you told me she was going to be here!
> Parent: Sorry, things changed.
> Kid: What about Molly? Can't she come watch her?

Parent: Babysitters are expensive. I need you to help me out.
Kid: Ugh. Okay. Which days? Derrick and I were supposed to play basketball tomorrow, and I wanted to go see that new scary movie this week.
Parent: What's it rated?
Kid: PG-13.
Parent: Which day were you planning to go?
Kid: Probably Thursday.
Parent: So you want Molly here tomorrow and Thursday?
Kid: Can I check with Derrick first?
Parent: Sure, just let me know as soon as possible.
Kid: I'll ask him right now.

Easy and considerate. The kid knew the mom could have dictated when he would have to stay home, or forced him to babysit every day. But the parent chose collaboration, which portrays respect for the relationship. This type of connected approach helps set an overall positive tone for the household.

Some parents worry that taking a partnership approach weakens the parent-child order and that the young human—who is naturally designed to occasionally push the envelope—will try to take advantage of the situation and cross a "hierarchal boundary." When and if the kid does attempt to establish an air of equal footing by doing something like telling instead of asking, cussing at home, trying to inappropriately joke with the parents like they're good buddies, or calling the parents by their first names, you can briskly end that baloney. Very respectfully, issue a strong reminder and hopefully that does the trick. But, if unsuitable behavior continues, there will be a consequence.

And feel free to occasionally sprinkle some humor throughout different areas of your parenting if you'd like, especially if you detect some potential contention brewing. That way, you are still making your point while being pleasant, which persuades the kid to be less defensive and more receptive to the message, and brings that child back down to earth. I once heard a mom in my office respond to her eight-year-old who was complaining about consequences:

> Kid: Why do I always have to do what you say? And you never get mad, you just make me do stuff, and I get in trouble if I don't.
> Mom: Are my expectations fair?
> Kid: Uh, I guess.
> Mom: And if you're able to have fun and still do what's expected (as the mom playfully pokes her kid's ribs and uses a funny voice), is life much better for you?
> Kid: Yeah.
> Mom: How about (she throws her hand up and does a Hamlet impersonation), "Yes, most honorable and perfect mother of all time."
> Kid smiles and shakes her head: Yes.
> *Greatness.*

Confident

If the kid you've raised for eighteen-years is genuinely self-confident, positive, forward-moving, and well-adjusted, you have successfully completed your most important mission in life. There is no feeling more comforting than knowing the human you were responsible for is headed to young adulthood as prepared as possible. Go ahead and pat yourself on the back because you played *the* premier role in this. And the fact that "Confident" is only one of five chapter headings in this book indicates how important this state of being is.

Let me tell you some reasons it's critical for humans to feel good about themselves. Self-confident and humble people seem to enjoy life more, have better relationships, create healthy boundaries, conquer challenges, do not give up easily, refrain from being needy, and consonantly strive for success. They're warm and affable. They don't take themselves too seriously, settle for mediocrity, or make things about them because they don't have to.

They get through the hard times and manage adversity as well as anybody. They accept responsibility, become leaders, do not make excuses, choose healthy ways to feel significant, advocate for themselves, and they aren't co-dependent. Genuinely confident humans don't intentionally hurt themselves or other people. They don't do overly crazy, inappropriate, and dangerous things as teenagers and adults because they're heavily invested in life and in the relationships they have with others. Therefore, as the parent who has an enormous influence on your children's overall level of fortitude, you will always be asking yourself, "Am I currently interacting in a way that's either neutral or somehow advancing my kids' self-worth? Or am I... not?"

Hmm.

Confidence Killers

As we all know, challenges loom for us parents working to keep it together for nearly two decades and get our kids soundly equipped to the launchpad. For many of us, the hardest thing about parenting effectively is consistently overriding two huge features that make us human: emotions (adverse ones) and "egoism," which states that deep down, we are always motivated to fulfill our own self-interest.

Other people (including our children) can cause us to feel negative. And regarding egoism, if we're driven to meet our own wants and needs first, that particular human instinct can drastically hinder us from meeting others' essential needs, including our children's. In other words, to be an excellent parent, we must learn to control these powerful, innate characteristics. Extremely difficult.

We have discussed in great detail the harm in feeling unfavorably towards our child, and we've also mentioned how this human selfishness thing keeps us from effectively enacting the two primary parental tasks. If we allow our negative feelings to be a significant player, then we poison the crucial relationship upon which *all good parenting is built*. If we are unable to meet our child's needs over our own wants and needs, then we cannot adequately protect and successfully advance our youngster; thus, the kid will inevitably run into enormous developmental trouble. Again, the first eighteen years of life are all about development, and as one travels through childhood and adolescence, one needs to be guided by self-assurance, not contaminated with self-doubt.

What all kids ultimately require is orthodox: the parents' love, acceptance, and approval with no conditions attached. But if we do not make that a well-established principle, then we're forcing our children to deal with a litany of problems. Initially, kids perceive their parents like demi-gods, and if those mighty figures interact destructively towards their naive children in various ways throughout the early years, then those little people assume something is wrong with themselves, since the formidable caregiver(s) most certainly cannot be at fault.

So, let's start with this confidence killer because this unintentional parenting *faux pas* is super common: telling our children how they "should" think or feel about things. No one has the right to dictate that. For example, "Oh come on—I know you like band." or "I can't believe you're so upset!" or "What's wrong with you? Don't you like to trick-or-treat?"

Instead: get patient, minimize your parental anxiety, and issue a response that allows the kiddo to work out the issue. "What's going on with band?" or "You seem upset about that." or "What do you want to do about Halloween?" This might be a hard habit for some of you to break, but I encourage you to do what you must to fix it.

Listen to your kid, take a minute or two to show respect through a conversation instead of immediately dictating how *you think* your child should feel, and help that young person create independent solutions. In other words, *slow down* and try to talk it through, like in the earlier example in Chapter 3 of the daughter wanting to quit tennis. The mom could have thoughtlessly blurted, "What are you talking about? You like tennis! You're good at it, and think of all the money we've spent on lessons!" But instead, this mother demonstrated respect, investigated the issue, determined her kid was legitimately done with that sport, and partnered with her to create another healthy physical option. This, again, met the parental goal: to appropriately develop her child.

I know most parents who administer the "Here's how you should feel" controlling technique are not doing it maliciously, but if we're going to be honest, it's shaming and manipulative. Also know, if a person is constantly told one's own thoughts or feelings are not acceptable, then something must be wrong, and self-acceptance is torpedoed.

One cannot feel confident without self-acceptance, as everything in our world and how we operate is significantly based on how we feel about ourselves. Significantly.

So if the messages from the parent are regularly infused with either blatant or underlying disapproval (or any of the other negative parenting aspects we've discussed), then the skewed child spends a needless amount of time and energy trying to somehow overcome what a dysfunctional parenting style generates, instead of having a proper home environment to work on self-awareness, self-identity, determination, and self-discipline. The daily communication strategies you execute will create a landscape of either healthy self-growth, or chronic self-uncertainty. Fostering confidence is a Tri-C fundamental principle that must be diligently addressed as you consistently place enormous value on everything that comes out of your mouth. A careless or arrogant parent creates senseless, underlying damage to the child.

Also, as mentioned earlier, a young human cannot withstand frosty disengagement or the ridiculous bombardment of constant criticism. To develop properly, the child actually needs the *exact opposite*; which means, "What does my child appropriately need from me right now?" Which usually means to "talk with" instead of being disrespectful. Countless sessions in my office involve me trying to convince the parent(s) to set aside their frustration or anxiety, and effectively perform the job they signed up for. Because when selfishness, frustration, and anxiety are allowed to become the parents' puppet masters, the child woefully suffers.

Anxiety: Because I'm a clinician who understands the rampant nature of anxiety amongst humans and the gravity of its negative effects, I want you parents to be privy to this information. There's a decent chance one of your kids might be struck by it.

Anxiety is the heavyweight champion of all mental issues. The National Alliance on Mental Illness and the National Institute of Mental Health report more people struggle with anxiety than with all other diagnoses. And in regard to self-confidence, it's the Mike Tyson beat-down of all behavioral health beat-downs.

I've treated numerous youngsters with anxiety who look great on paper: smart, nice-looking, creative, personable, athletic, good family, etc., but their self-esteem is in the toilet. Why? Because as anxiety goes up, confidence goes down. Let me explain. We humans are not necessarily in control of what goes on around us; therefore, we very much need to be in control of what goes on inside us, meaning our thoughts and feelings. Our thoughts (the ones which actually require our focus) must be rational, pragmatic, and controllable, and we need to be able to regulate our feelings effectively.

Anxiety almost always starts right out of the gate at birth and comes in a wide variety of symptoms. In other words, it can impact humans in many different ways. How it impacts self-worth: if someone is debilitated by excessive worries, or overthinks certain issues all the time, or if too many irrational cognitions are constantly distorting thoughts and grinding down the individual, then that person feels exhausted and out of control. If a person regularly feels out of control, then self-doubt becomes a significant player. That human unfortunately begins to incessantly question oneself, dwell on difficulties, and over-amplify troubles. That is not a healthy mental terrain for self-confidence, which should be loaded with stability, self-assurance, and rational perceptions of self and of the world. Thoughts need to be accurately processed so functioning can be normal.

Clinical anxiety tends to increase as children get older, and humans (who *hate* to feel anxious) develop coping mechanisms to deal with their issues. Sometimes kids' coping mechanisms are harmful (e.g., self-injury, eating disorders, drug/alcohol abuse, reckless behavior), and the more the dysfunctional behaviors run the show, the more acceptable it becomes to be out of control. Not good. It is never permissible to normalize dysfunctional behavior. Anxiety and negative actions can also lead to depressive symptoms. Do not hesitate to seek professional help or some type of resource if your kid's problems have risen to the degree they can't be resolved at home.

Acceptance and Electronics

This chapter is not terribly long because the overall approach of Tri-C (which you have now learned quite a bit about) heavily promotes confidence throughout. So let's take a look at what may seem to be an odd pairing in the confidence-building department: acceptance and electronics. Regarding acceptance, we've got two primary parts here: acceptance from the parents and acceptance from peers. Both huge. Clearly it begins with parents. We've discussed plenty regarding the value of parental acceptance of the child, so let's talk about peers.

Kids needs friends and face-to-face social interactions. This is irreplaceable. For extroverted youngsters who possess strong social skills, this task is relatively easy to meet. There is an internal force pressing outgoing individuals to interact more fully. Obviously, the more we engage in something and the more practice we get, the more masterful we become, and this includes making real friends and learning to effectively connect with others. However, kids who tend to be more introverted or lacking somewhat in interpersonal skills absolutely *must* have social repetition. For shy or quirky children, electronic devices have become public enemy #1.

I'm not stating that the internet and all things virtual are bad; this modern way to function in so many areas of human existence is astounding and now necessary. However, we have provided our youth a medium that has become way too captivating. How in the world can we expect our children to be responsible with technology when there are countless adults who cannot manage electronics in a responsible fashion? (I highly encourage no fixed devices in kids' bedrooms, including televisions and desktops—it is too difficult to oversee what they're viewing/playing and their actual time spent online.)

Children can expose themselves to inappropriate material (including certain video games) and navigate through online milieus they simply are not mature enough to handle, including pornography and various social media apps, which give our impressionable youngsters distorted, toxic messages.

Many parents are also guilty of permitting way too much screen time (including on phones) that delivers kids into the electronic world to endlessly disappear, which unfortunately prevents them from the important opportunities to develop the social and life skills they so desperately need. With that being said, interacting virtually does have some value, but it absolutely can't replace the worth of consistently being in the physical presence of others as one learns to build deep, meaningful friendships, receive critical feedback, and deal with all kinds of people in all types of situations.

One of the most well-known research projects on nonverbal communication was led by Dr. Mehrabian in the 1960s. He concluded the interpretation of a message is 7 percent verbal, 38 percent "tone/delivery," and 55 percent visual, meaning 93 percent of communication is nonverbal in nature.

Because there's a good argument that a considerable amount of human success in life hinges on the ability to relate well to others and become a well-rounded individual, then letting children spend an inordinate amount of time glued to a screen does significant harm to personal development, which violates one of the primary parental tasks. In other words, as parents, we must limit our kids' time on devices, help them pursue their worthwhile personal interests, and dutifully police (the other parental task: to protect) what's being viewed, particularly social media—get educated on this and its potentially destructive nature. When we were little kids, our folks did not let us watch R-rated movies on cable or sit in front of the TV all day and night (although sometimes we tried to get away with it).

"I'm bored..." our kids will moan after we've said, "Time is up." Tell them to grab a broom, and watch them miraculously find something else to do. It is not your job to entertain your children, especially once they're in third grade. It's okay to partner with your kids to generate some options, but do not feel like it is your pronounced responsibility. They will ultimately seek other ways to spend their time (maybe even with family!) and hopefully a decent amount will be distributed to being with other kids in some social undertaking, from sports, to dance, to music, to something creative, to cruising around the neighborhood. Older kids might need to find a job (especially in the summer) if they aren't in hyper-competitive sports or activities.

And speaking of sports or competitive extracurriculars: these contain monumental value. Your children do not have to be all-world at whatever they are engaged in, but we learn so much about ourselves and life in so many ways through competition. This is not limited to sports; there is competition in art, theater, academics, etc.

Yes, you do need to make sure your child or adolescent stays physically active, but not all humans are good athletes. Since the holy trinity of self-administered wellness is **good sleep, a healthy diet, and regular exercise**, as a responsible parent upholding the primary parental tasks, you cannot compromise on this. You must do all you can to "make" your kid meet all three of these consistently until your child is old enough to take the reins. Essentially, we have eighteen years to try to appropriately "condition" our kid to become self-responsible and hope our influence was effectively delivered. Virtual world is the nemesis of the "holy trinity," and I don't want to waste your time and tell you why.

If your kid rocks at a sport or some type of competitive physical pastime, great! The child is being active, developing a healthy identity, interacting with other kids, and learning self-discipline, teamwork, and how to deal with defeat—all skills which help build self-confidence. But again, not every kid is athletic, so now we're talking about making sure the child is engaged in some degree of consistent physical exertion while actively competing in some type of medium. This goes hand-in-hand with limited screen time. Opportunities abound when electronic ecstasy is appropriately tempered and not used as the convenient babysitter (guilty as charged!) or as the child's primary source of engagement.

As alluded to earlier, two hours of recreational screen time on school days as long as all responsibilities are being met, along with five to six hours a day on weekends (unless it's a special occasion or a creative project) sounds very reasonable and will certainly prompt the kid to find other things to do. Five to six hours on a Saturday or Sunday including during summer may sound like a lot, but if your kid sleeps nine hours, that still leaves up to nine hours for non-electronic activities. (Also, let the kid decide how to spend fun screen time, e.g., four hours on Play Station and two hours on the laptop, and this includes staring at the phone.) Realize you might have to consistently police and reinforce this protocol until your child potentially demonstrates self-responsibility. This might sound exhausting, but again, consistency and commitment are irreplaceable anchors of good parenting.

I've treated a generous number of offbeat kids who've temporarily lost their technology privileges due to some infraction. The parents then tell me how much more personably and "normally" their kid is acting. What's happened is the young human is not suffering from "online intoxication," and understands there is no hypnotic, virtual world to plummet into where it's safe, fun, and easy to disregard expectations. The child now has invaluable opportunities to personally interact with others in the real world and develop other areas of functioning, and is more open to meeting real-world requirements.

Allowing too much screen time also prevents our kids from effectively growing their full imagination and creativity. The virtual world is simply too enticing: they get instantly sucked in, hour after hour, day after day, and experience unnatural, chronic dopamine rushes from the bombardment of irresistible digital stimulation. *"My youngster has the attention span of a gnat! I can't even get this kid to play a board game or sit through an awesome, classic movie!"* The harmful, shallow fulfillment provided from online activity has addictive properties, which entices children to continually be reabsorbed when they could instead be actively participating in real-world, meaningful ventures, and substantially developing their important skill sets and creative minds.

Therefore, limiting technology has two powerful confidence-building elements. One, you generate the mandatory time your child needs to broaden and strengthen other areas of life. Two, because humans are a herding species and we require meaningful relationships with others (three-dimensional friends, not just two-dimensional), your child's social skills will likely advance because the kid must now connect with others offline, not just online. If the most attractive human characteristic is confidence, your kid feels more self-assured as personal strengths and social dexterity are continually afforded the time to mature. Well guess what? This will impress some peers. Now you think your kid is great, and your kid will have real friends who feel the same.

Although your child will certainly run up against some bullies (physical and virtual) and other tough players along the way, genuine, steady social interaction will create a friend group (small, medium, or large—depends on how introverted or extraverted you kid is) to hang with and help your child feel accepted, develop richness in life, learn about self and others more intimately, and provide important peer support whenever needed. Listen, I'm dead serious about this friend thing. A kid must feel desired by some peers. If your child is ten years old or older and does not seem to have at least a few good buddies, you've got to investigate that. Again, identify what type of young human you've got, find your kid's tribe, and create the opportunities for your child to start cultivating some authentic friendships.

I cannot put a high enough price tag on having real friends and diversified strengths and interests. I know some of you reading this book have got a somewhat eccentric kid who will howl when you limit time on devices and press for more healthy engagements. But, unless you uphold hard protocols regarding technology, a reserved youngster who lacks somewhat in initiative can completely submerge if allowed. (Quick suggestion: No phones or electronics at the dinner table or when you're out to eat. And this means *all* family members.)

Again, the key is "appropriate" time spent. You are trying to help your child achieve some balance. I'm not sure what more I can say about the virtual world, nor can I propose a different way to stress this mainstay of good parenting. As crazy as this sounds, minimizing screen time might very well be your most important and greatest challenge as a parent.

Trust

When you demonstrate you trust your kid, it helps promote confidence. You're sending the message that you're convinced your child can handle whatever the situation is, and you trust good decisions will be made overall. Some parents have a solid youngster who does a nice job checking nearly all the "responsible" boxes, but they still micro-manage excessively. Whether it's from needless suspicion or too much control, the parents are always looking over the trustworthy child's shoulder. "Let me see your phone." "What are you doing up in your room?" "You need to try harder." "You better not drive too fast because you know I track you." The list of unwarranted orders goes on and on.

Again, most parents are merely trying to be good caregivers and to shape their child to make good choices, but they discount how imperative it is to be strategic about when a necessary vs. unnecessary message is delivered. Why do some parents grapple with this? *Because I'm an adult and you're just a clueless kid, and I can say whatever I want and treat you however I want, and I honor my anxiety and wants more than your development.* Protecting and developing are entrenched in most parents' minds, but as you now understand, Tri-C is passionately about the correct way to fulfill these two commissions.

Yes, for us parents it is much easier to "tell" instead of allowing ourselves to loosen up a little, ask a rhetorical question, or engage in a considerate conversation. Because if we command our child or needlessly repeat orders over and over, our assumption is the kid will robotically accept our demands and blindly obey out of respect—*I'm the parent who knows, and you're the child who doesn't*—and we don't want to have to explain or feel worried or potentially argue. Well, guess what? That what's called disrespectful.

So for the kid, the young "employee" on the receiving end of unnecessary dominance, not only does this generate negative feelings towards the "boss" (we know that's bad), but also an authoritarian approach must indicate the parent does not trust the young human, who must primarily rely on the all-powerful overlord for either approval or instructions on making decisions. This sends the child the message "You must not be capable and apparently cannot count on yourself to steer your life correctly" or "You're always doing something wrong." A kid who isn't allowed to navigate life to the proper degree is not allowed to adequately build self-confidence.

As we discussed earlier, most parents who over-control do it out of selfish dismissiveness *(I should get to say whatever I want and parent however I want*) or excess anxiety. This is not easy to remedy. But you must. As your child gets older, you must train yourself to be respectful and to not intervene unless you absolutely have to. Take just a second to analyze different situations and determine if your intervention will help or hurt childhood development.

Of course you will intercede if there's imminent danger or a disastrous mistake in the making, or if you clearly recognize your child isn't getting it or absolutely needs your mature guidance to achieve a goal or meet an expectation. Remember, a grand majority of raising a child is nothing more than seeing if the kid demonstrates the ability to meet a responsibility.

If you find yourself barking instructions and "talking at" your youngster all the time, you're also watering down your parenting. In other words: *Show me you can take care of business, i.e., put your dishes in the dishwasher, eat more healthy foods, or do your homework. Because the fewer words I have to use when parenting, the more meaningful they are, and the less I have to order or remind you.*

And here's something else to earnestly consider: when you appropriately allow your child more independence and the opportunities for the real world to teach life lessons, not only do those experiences tend to be super powerful, you're also taken off the hook as the too-controlling caregiver. *(My job is to set you up for success, not guarantee your success.)* We all learn many things the hard way because we're supposed to. Permit your child to learn some things the hard way, too. Nearly everything can be fixed.

The positive, safe, and accepting culture of your household also advances self-confidence, and the constant message of "how great you are" (but not false praise) and how much you love your kid adds to self-worth. I see parents who are misled in their thinking and who feel the best way to toughen up their child is to run the house military-style. This approach makes it very difficult to create a connected relationship. Home is not boot camp and you are not a drill sergeant; you are the devoted mom or dad. Home is the safe haven of love, fun, stability, and respect. Your job is to lift your child up, not tear your child down. The world will do its best to pummel your kid; do not contribute to that garbage.

Up, up, up, always up! Never down! Never criticize! Promote self-acceptance. Promote self-confidence. Reinforce self-worth. Always. The better kids feel about themselves, the more they are willing to set goals, accept challenges, push themselves, take healthy risks, and feel empowered.

The more someone is fueled to achieve, the more that human will engage in challenging endeavors, and that will humble and toughen up your kid aplenty. There are abundant amounts of competitive opportunities for your bold child to experience, and your child's boldness is inexhaustibly fostered by—guess who?—*you*. Tri-C style: Respect. Acceptance. Love. Confidence. You know you're doing great as a parent when you randomly say to your kid, "You're awesome," and your child replies, "I know."

Complete

Home stretch! As you complete your mission of great parenting, the final few years look very different from any other period of child-rearing. If your kid has reached late adolescence and you've been a Tri-C rock star, this phase is easy. You are consistent and selfless, and you do not waver on expectations being met. You complete your appropriate parenting tasks every day, constantly stay relatable, and advance self-worth and self-responsibility. However, if your child is an older teen and this is your initial exposure to *The Way*, it is paramount for you to interact with utmost respect, uphold the two primary parental tasks (protect and develop), and stay completely in charge.

You still have all the power, and the adolescent knows it. I had an affable dad and his moderately rigid sixteen-year-old son in my office. The father was trying to convince the stubborn teen to go to bed on school nights at a reasonable hour, as the kid disrespectfully tried to convince the dad he should get to do what he wants. This apparently had been going on since the start of the school year. As I listened to this I thought *Why is this dad putting up with this, and why is he still "asking" his kid to get off his phone and go to sleep? And for that matter, why in the heck does he have his phone in his room on school nights, especially when he continues to demonstrate he cannot be responsible and go to bed at a decent hour?*

Once the father stepped out, I said, "Man, your dad sure is nice. Why doesn't he just take your phone?"

"I dunno," he shrugged. "I guess he doesn't want me to get mad."

I responded, "So what if you do?"

The kid gave me a flat look, then after a second, smirked and said, "I dunno."

The dad was afraid of his son getting angry? Really? Paired with unrealistic expectations? As in *I trust (hope) you'll stop speeding if I just keep asking you to slow down?*

On the other hand, I see parents who keep swinging the power saber all throughout upbringing for whatever reason (arrogance? frustration?) to demonstrate dominance and try to force the kid to be more compliant. But once late adolescence arrives, a teen raised in that fashion is typically so disillusioned that the crucial parent-child relationship is in the trash. *I know I'm your child, but you have no credibility with me. You never even tried to understand me or be respectful...*

Here's the thing with this final chapter. You now know how much of this parenting system works. In the situation described above between the super-nice dad and his brooding son, my guess is as you were reading, you already had in mind how you would properly handle it. And for overly commanding parents, it is still not too late. Tri-C is standing by.

Vaping / Marijuana / Alcohol—The Big Three

Sooner than later, your kid will go from a six- to a sixteen-year-old or already has, and what a difference ten years can make. We parents all knew one day our innocent child who proudly held hands with us walking to elementary school, regularly crawled in our lap, excitedly ran everywhere, and let us wipe jelly off that sweet little face would eventually develop into a teenager. But if you had informed us that after tucking our little angel into bed with a good-night kiss, following an evening game of *Chutes and Ladders,* that our precious child would evolve into some unrecognizable version of an intolerable adolescent whom we continually caught vaping, or smoking marijuana, or drinking, we would've been horrified.

Which leads me to this: Teenagers' experimentation with wrongdoings are relatively normal and have been happening for a long time, so do not be shocked if you catch yours. Although a decent number of adolescents do not partake to any degree, when and if you do discover chemical mischievousness, there are meaningful implications in how that first *"You're busted!"* is handled. Remember, you do not want to damage the relationship, you want to see what the real deal is behind it, and you want to make sure the kid ultimately stops doing it. Within the conversation (20 second spurts), you will state you do not expect it to happen again. But sometimes it does happen again.

First: why? Because teens are curious, and they sometimes want to be like an adult or some of their friends. Let's say you've got a good kid who does quite well at life, but you catch the young thrill-seeker dabbling a very small number of times throughout high school. You do not detect any abuse or dependency—just a matter of your kid feeling a little peer pressure or being moronic/social/devious. What's the one-two punch that keeps solid kids from entertaining the idea that habitually smoking or drinking is acceptable? Confidence and awareness, and coming from an adolescent, it sounds something like this:

Because if I'm truly confident (not arrogant or cocky), then I feel good about myself. I authentically feel good about myself because my folks are heavily invested in me. They cultivated my strengths and uncompromisingly provided me the means to boldly develop. I do not have to give in to unhealthy ways to cope with life, or falsely represent myself. Although I'm just a teenager who believes I'm mostly bulletproof, I know drugs (including nicotine) and alcohol are bad for kids' brains and bodies, I do not want to disappoint my parents, my close friends do not use regularly (we are who our friends are, especially during high school), and I do not want illegal activities derailing the satisfying life I have established.

Okay Brian, but what about a "good" kid from a "good" home who does appear to regularly vape or use marijuana or drink alcohol? Here's how that happens. That unfortunate young human most likely wasn't doing as well as the parents had thought. And maybe the parents weren't quite as dialed in as they could've been. Aside from the normal teenager-parent disconnect, certain youngsters are skillful at disguising some personal troubles and hiding contraband.

Vaping: Kids who like to vape saw some peers do it and thought it looked impressive. So they try it. It tastes good, they feel cool (yet initially conflicted), and they catch a quick nicotine buzz. *Uh-oh.* Nicotine is physiologically addictive. The more we do it, the more our cells crave it. Now they think they *need* it.

But in the meantime, *what's up with my kid who even thought it was okay to vape?* As the parent who will not freak out, you can begin exploring by asking—you guessed it—"Why?" then objectively focusing on the issue(s), whether it's curiosity, immaturity/cluelessness, peer pressure, or the alarming reasons: negative self-esteem and poor coping skills.

After briefly discussing (not lecturing) the dangers, and beginning the process of doing what's necessary to effectively address whatever the youngster might be struggling with (especially if it is something bigger than mere experimentation), you will initiate a one-week grounding from everything. Kid can go to school and team-oriented activities (as you won't punish teammates), but other than that, zero privileges. No screens, including phone and TV, no car, and no friends. Your child can read books, play with sticks in the backyard, you don't care, but that's it.

If busted again, a two-week grounding, then nicotine tests twice a week until you're convinced usage has stopped. As the responsible parent, you'll partner with your child to resolve the initial matter that persuaded said kid to vape, and you'll execute reasonable consequences that will compel your child to stop. A "good" kid (or any kid for that matter), has no business sucking on a vape device. You also understand groundings can be hugely inconvenient for you, but you will not compromise these measures or lecture along the way. Remember, no cracks in your parenting wall, and the consequences will do the talking for you. Firmly maintain healthy standards (guardrails), no matter what. Your child can not afford for you to shortchange your parenting in any capacity.

Marijuana: The CDC and the American Academy of Child and Adolescent Psychiatry report adolescent cannabis use is higher (no pun intended) than ever: close to half of all high school kids admit to having used marijuana. Although widely accepted in many social circles and growing in legalization (again, no pun intended), current research is informing us that long-term use increases risk of psychosis, early onset of Alzheimer's, depression, and suicidal ideation. Not good.

Marijuana is best buddies with apathy and escape. Most individuals, when high, are not too interested in much other than being high. And because marijuana is insidious and does not police itself like alcohol (can't get away with being drunk constantly), people can avoid reality and smoke almost every day if they so choose. They can stay chill and go undetected as they perform minimal expectations at work or school, wake up the next day, experience no hangover, and do it all over again. Once marijuana sinks its cunning claws into many of its victims, dependency takes over, and productivity goes in the dumpster.

Teenagers are in the business of developing their natural coping mechanisms which prepare them for adulthood when life gets more difficult. For vulnerable kids whose irresponsible parents "tolerate" them getting high, these youngsters are not sufficiently provided the opportunity for coping mechanisms to expand. I've had countless 19- to 22-year-olds in my office who finally realized their moderate to heavy pot use throughout their teenage years arrested their development, as valuable opportunities to deal with life issues were hijacked by the drug. Many are immature, insecure, and self-loathing. Many realize the majority of their friendships were not real. They see their functioning peers "miles ahead of them" and are left to battle a powerful emotional addiction that prevented them from experiencing normal and developmental pain that naturally motivates humans to strive. People hate to feel any type of pain and will do what must be done to relieve it, either by escape or by implementation of change, also known as growth. *Self-growth: good. Self-medication: bad.*

I had an honest dad of two non-using teenagers in my office. We were discussing the growing popularity of cannabis use. To paraphrase, he said something like, "Regardless of the country's population, there's only so much room at the top. If these 'Gen Z' kids (ages 9–24 at the time of publication) think it's okay to get high, well, that just makes it all the easier for my kids to be successful."

Tri-C consequences you will execute if you catch your kid with weed include the "why" and hazards conversation, followed by a full-blown, two-week grounding of everything, and I mean everything. A kid can find solace in the smallest of perks, like getting to watch TV or taking a smart phone to school because "I need it." No, your child does not need it. Get that kid a flip phone to use during school hours only if you must communicate for some legitimate reason.

If caught smoking again at any time within a month or two, there might be a problem—not sure yet. Issue again the two-week grounding, but now include random drug tests. It typically takes two to three weeks for marijuana to leave someone's system unless usage was heavy, and if it was, then you're looking at up to six weeks to test clean. If the child cannot pass or you continue to detect usage, especially after you've made the struggling youngster's life absolutely dismal a few different times, then there most likely is an actual issue. Find a good therapist, community advocacy center, or look into treatment programs. Regardless of all the preposterous propaganda your adolescent will try to sell you, do not allow marijuana to become a player in your child's life. An emotionally fragile kid can be too immature and vulnerable to avoid its nefarious seduction. It has no place, especially during this critical period of brain and life-skill development.

Alcohol: Not designed to be used regularly, but designed to be used recreationally. And not designed for kids. I know parents who "sort of" let their older teens drink but this is a slippery slope, and in all honesty, I do not have a universal answer. In some European countries, people are permitted to drink at a relatively early age. Is this a good thing? I'm not sure. Does it help older adolescents "learn" how to consume more responsibly? Research gives mixed results. Also, it's prohibited in the U.S. for people under twenty-one-years-old, and comes with a high price tag if caught by legal authorities (same with marijuana).

If your kid frightfully develops a drinking habit, you will know, as adults can't hide a drinking habit. You cannot allow it to continue. Alcoholism is real, and I do not think I need to inform you what that horror show is all about. You might permit your adolescent to occasionally drink at parties, but if it becomes any semblance of a regular thing, then you are not upholding the primary parental tasks, which again, are priority number one. The safest approach is a no-tolerance policy—just saying.

If you apprehend your child drunk or with alcohol, do not freak out. Have a brief, strong talk, then enact the hardline, two-week sentence. If it happens again within six to twelve months, slap that kid with another two-week grounding. But if alcohol infractions continue to mount, you've lost control or there's a bigger problem. It might be time to seek outside help.

There certainly are solid kids who struggle with personal difficulties and never turn to substances, but because marijuana, alcohol, and vape devices are so readily obtainable and condoned amongst numerous teens, the door is more open today than ever. Therefore, as the parent, please recognize that an adolescent *knows* it is illegal and wrong to drink or smoke (or consume any drug), and if regular usage of any chemical vice is present, you'll need to A) understand why the kid feels motivated to consume, and B) obviously take action to address the issue. But if your youngster is simply being a normal yet dopey teenager and is trying to get away with something stupid, then you'll convincingly put the screws to that naive human. In other words, "I won't be responsible for you after you move out and become an adult, but this ain't happening on my watch."

Stress

Be careful about how much strain your teenager can handle, as too much stress is poison to healthy childhood development. If your kid is self-directed, then your ambitious, responsible-acting child is likely applying plenty of personal pressure to achieve—your role might simply be as a wise consultant. Remember, you are constantly striving to find the parental balance between when to step in, and when to let the young person figure out "whatever it is" independently, as you work to prevent your anxiety from overruling your ability to parent with an objective mind.

Our world is becoming more competitive every day, and you certainly want your child to do well. What's frustrating for many parents is when they recognize their somewhat lackadaisical kid is smart or athletic or talented in the arts, but clearly lacks initiative. Parents are confounded by this, and I see this a lot.

What's needed is some parental "leaning." But parents must be careful as they differentiate "leaning into" someone and "pushing" someone. Nobody likes to be pushed. Pushing tends to backfire, anyway. Partnering, holding conversations (not lectures), and reinforcing a hard-working family protocol is the Tri-C way to recognize and grow the child's strengths.

Again, your child's strengths need to be developed to build self-confidence and a healthy identity. Do not compromise on this undertaking no matter what, as it falls under one of your primary parental tasks. (If your kid tends to be more of a jack of all trades, then instead of seeing a dedicated amount of effort towards only one or two pursuits, you should see steady, present demonstrations of involvement in a number of different healthy activities throughout childhood and adolescence.)

For older kids, the area where we unfortunately see parents tending to overdo it is academics. As we know (but sometimes disregard), life mostly begins after college or after our mid-20s when we finally learn how to be adults. Yes, it's more difficult these days to get into a stellar university, and yes, some initial employers are paying more attention to GPAs, but overall prosperity in life is determined by what we do *after* college and after we have been on our own for a while, not necessarily where we went to school, how long it took us to graduate, or what our GPA was.

Confidence, connections, and a strong work ethic will almost always get us where we want to go.

Unless your child plans to do something spectacular like work for NASA, go to Harvard Medical School, be an investment banker on Wall Street, or get a scholarship to play Division 1 college ball followed by a realistic shot at the pros, how critical is it for your kid to go to an "elite" college? And for that matter, how many actual "bad" colleges are there? Clearly, it is important for our kid to understand the value in making good grades, but do we punish our middle- or high-schooler for not making straight A's? And do we radiate disappointment if our kid doesn't make the "A" team or first chair or land the lead role?

My point is: your teenager or tween is still just a kid. Time to relax and have fun is a must, because that wonderful luxury as a regular thing will inevitably come to an end. So ask yourself, "Am I appropriately partnering with my kid or appropriately leaning, or does my heavy determination to push my child stem from my own anxiety or personal desires?"

Being a Tri-C parent, you strongly value the Connected Way relationship, which means you are incredibly interested in listening to your youngster, honoring how your kid feels with conversations not lectures, finding the sweet spot of effective parenting by managing or helping your child appropriately develop, and knowing who that person is. So if your child needs you to "lean," then feel free; just make sure not to force or create burn out.

Here's what lots of parents say: "What stinks about today's world is that when my child does have free time, instead of spending it engaged in what appears to be more healthy or productive activities, my kid is staring at a screen—ugh!" This maddening dynamic clearly makes it easier to justify pushing the child to study more or practice more.

If that's the case, because that kid is demonstrating the choice to not use free time more constructively, then firmly enact the recreational screen time protocol of only two hours on school days (as long as all responsibilities are being met), and five to six hours a day on weekends. And regarding tweens and teenagers, it absolutely is not your responsibility to entertain or pacify that person. You can make some suggestions regarding other activities, but don't get suckered or become a pushover when your kid tries to guilt or bully you about "needing" more time on devices. And realize that if your kid does become significantly involved in some kind of substantial extracurricular, screen time will automatically minimize by default!

Future

Although not universal, there are five relatively common options upon high school graduation:

1. Go to a four-year university. If it's totally funded by parents and the kid wants to continue that arrangement, then parents typically require certain criteria, e.g., make good grades, don't get pregnant or get anyone pregnant, and do not get into any significant legal trouble.

2. Go to a trade school. If it's local, honor the parents' reasonable rules as an adult living in their house.

3. Go to a local community college, live at home, and honor the parents' reasonable rules as an adult living in their house. Either become a full-time student, or get a part-time job and take a few classes per semester until a determination is made as to what's next.

4. Go join the military.

5. Go get a full-time job, and sooner than later move out.

The end of adolescence tends to be a bittersweet time for parents. You've just spent eighteen years being responsible for another human on a daily basis, and those days are coming to a close. If this is your only child or the last to leave, you become the empty nester. (Life becomes about you again!) If you still have a few more ducks in waiting, then the oldest duckling, with whom you hopefully have a wonderful relationship, you will miss terribly upon departure.

If the military is beckoning, well, that phase of life is self-explanatory. If your kid is going to hang around for another year or two and work or do community college or trade school, "partner up" to create fair house rules for the young adult who is choosing to reside with you. And if the kid is leaving for college and is mature and responsible, then hopefully you feel confident that all collegiate hurdles can be handled. But if you've got justifiable concerns because your teen experienced or is currently experiencing some obvious difficulties, is going off to college right away the best idea?

College isn't going anywhere; however, there are parents who say, "Go get 'em!" and wish their unequipped adolescent good luck, cross their fingers, and hope everything will be okay. But to be fresh out of high school, leave home, and experience success at a university, one must be a solid individual and in the correct mindset:

I can be competent and functional away from my parent(s). I am responsible and can figure out how to balance my time. I've got to prioritize academics, then everything else comes after that. I might occasionally feel somewhat unsettled because I'm a new college student, but I think I know, or maybe don't know, exactly what I want to do for a living after graduation; however, I recognize the value in a degree and possess the abilities to do what I need to do to stay here.

If your kid hits these maturity marks, then the young academic should be in decent shape for independent college living. But what about the student who, somewhere along the way, does not adequately earn the right to continue to receive your financial support? I'm merely stating if you feel your child must leave for college at all costs, and if your concerns regarding sustained success are valid, then be prepared for a possible early exit from campus, followed by a return home for a year or two, getting a job immediately (do not compromise on this), possibly taking some community college classes, and experiencing an important developmental phase in maturity.

If your kid is either slow to launch or needs to make a home pit stop, all is not lost. You will essentially be the parent who appropriately supports the kid who is in limbo and will need to, and should be able to, "figure it out" sooner than later. You have more than likely groomed your child to know what ultimately needs to be done to eventually manufacture a fulfilling adult life, college or not. We can sit in the boat and offer some direction, but everyone has to paddle their own canoe. Your child is now on the verge of becoming a grown-up and will soon enter the realm of total self-responsibility. So no matter who or what your kid becomes or experiences along the way, your mission remains the same: to be the everlasting bedrock of appropriate support.

You know what? I think that's it! I hope this was helpful. This model has been in the works for a decade and a half, and hopefully I've refined it enough for you to effectively implement and fully enjoy parenthood. Again, do not be reluctant to reread certain chapters or sections if you feel it would be helpful. Like I said, bright, terrific parents occasionally come back to my office for follow-ups to revisit some of the Tri-C fundamentals. What a job it is to be a parent. Once a parent, always a parent. Your kid needs you now and always, and Tri-C will always be here for you.

Thanks again and God bless,
Brian

References

American Academy of Child and Adolescent Psychiatry. (2019, October) *Marijuana and Teens,* No. 106. https://www.aacap.org/AACAP/Families_and_Youth/Facts_for_Families/FFF-Guide/Marijuana-and-Teens-106.aspx

Britannica, T. Editors of Encyclopaedia (2020, May 5). *Stanford Prison Experiment*. Encyclopedia Britannica. https://www.britannica.com/event/Stanford-Prison-Experiment

Centers for Disease Control and Prevention. (2021, March 22) *Data and Statistics on Children's Mental Health.* https://www.cdc.gov/childrensmentalhealth/data.html

Centers for Disease Control and Prevention. (2017, April 13) *What You Need to Know About Marijuana Use in Teens.* https://www.cdc.gov/marijuana/factsheets/teens.htm

Cline, F. & Fay, F. (2006) *Parenting With Love and Logic.* Colorado Springs, CO: NavPress Publishing Group.

DeMille, C.B. (Director). (1956). *The Ten Commandments* [Film]. Cecil B. DeMille Productions.

Dobson, James C. (2004), *The New Strong-Willed Child.* Carol Stream, IL: Tyndale.

Favreau, J. (Writer), & Filoni, D. (Director). (2019, November 11). Chapter 1: The Mandalorian (Season 1, Episode 1) [TV Series]. In J. Favreau, D. Filoni, K. Kennedy (Executive Producers), *The Mandalorian.* Lucasfilm, Fairview Entertainment, Golem Entertainment.

Kemp, Carla (2018, November 5) *AAP recommends positive discipline rather than physical, verbal punishment*. AAP News. American Academy of Pediatrics. https://www.aappublications.org/news/2018/11/05/nce18discipline110518

Landreth, Garry L. (2002) *Play Therapy: The Art of the Relationship.* New York: Brunner-Routledge.

Mehrabian, Albert. (1972) *Nonverbal Communication.* United Kingdom: Taylor & Francis.

National Alliance on Mental Illness (2017, December) *Anxiety Disorders.* https://www.nami.org/About-Mental-Illness/Mental-Health-Conditions/Anxiety-Disorders

National Alliance on Mental Heatlh (2018, July) *Anxiety Disorders.* https://www.nimh.nih.gov/health/topics/anxiety-disorders

Scharf, Richard S. (2000) *Theories of Psychotherapy and Counseling.* Belmont, CA: Wadsworth.

Zeltser, Francyne (2021, June 29). *Raising Successful Kids.* CNBC. https://www.cnbc.com/2021/06/29/child-psychologist-explains-4-types-of-parenting-and-how-to-tell-which-is-right-for-you.html

About The Author

Dr. Brian Rees is a native North Texan, and grew up in the Dallas-Fort Worth Metroplex. While obtaining his Master's & PhD at the University of North Texas, Dr. Rees was running a mental health clinic, and instructing undergraduates and graduates in psychology and counseling courses. Then in 2007 he opened his private practice, primarily focused on therapy with tweens, adolescents, young adults, and their parents. After living the life of a lead singer in a rock band in his 20's, he is now trying to keep up with his wife & three daughters.

Dr. Rees is also a partner of a mediation service called Divorce Without Duress, and, the founder of Tri-C Parenting. After spending 15 years and over 40,000 hours counseling kids and their parents, he has created this fundamental and widely applicable system to help navigate the complex path of productive parenting.

Visit www.TriCParenting.com for more info.

If you enjoyed this book please leave a review & help me reach more readers like you!

Made in the USA
Coppell, TX
10 February 2022

73273152R00076